1300

MW00577921

ISBN 0-933546-42-4

9 780933 546424

KHANIQAHI-NIMATULLAHI
(NIMATULLAHI SUFI ORDER)

306 West 11th Street
New York, New York 10014
Tel: 212-924-7739

4021 19th Avenue
San Francisco,
California 94132
Tel: 415-586-1313

4931 MacArthur Blvd. NW
Washington, D.C. 20007
Tel: 202-338-4757

84 Pembroke Street
Boston,
Massachusetts 02118
Tel: 617-536-0076

310 NE 57th Street
Seattle, Washington 98105
Tel: 206-527-5018

11019 Arleta Avenue
Mission Hills,
Los Angeles,
California 91345
Tel: 818-365-2226

4642 North Hermitage
Chicago, Illinois 60640
Tel: 312-561-1616

405 Greg Avenue
Santa Fe, New Mexico 87501
Tel: 505-983-8500

219 Chace Street
Santa Cruz, California 95060
Tel: 408-425-8454

95 Old Lansdowne Road
West Didsbury, Manchester
M20 8N2, England
Tel: 061-434-8857

Kölner Strasse 176
5000 Köln 90 (Porz)
Federal Republic of Germany
Tel: 49-2203-15390

Van Blankenburgstraat 66b
2517 XS's-Gravenhage,
The Netherlands
Tel: 070-450251

50 Rue du 4em Zouaves
Rosny-sous-Bois
Paris, France
Tel: 48552809

63 Boulevard Latrille
BP 1224 Abidjan,
CIDEX 1 Côte d'Ivoire
Tel. 225-410510

41 Chepstow Place
London W2 4TS,
England
Tel: 071-229-0769

SUFI WOMEN

Also available by Dr. Javad Nurbakhsh:

1. In the Tavern of Ruin: Seven Essays on Sufism
2. In the Paradise of the Sufis
3. What the Sufis Say
4. Masters of the Path
5. Divani Nurbakhsh: Sufi Poetry
6. Sufism (I): Meaning, Knowledge and Unity
7. Traditions of the Prophet, Vol. I
8. Sufism (II): Fear and Hope, Contraction and Expansion, Gathering and Dispersion, Intoxication and Sobriety, Annihilation and Subsistence
9. The Truths of Love: Sufi Poetry
10. Sufi Women
11. Traditions of the Prophet, Vol. II
12. Jesus in the Eyes of the Sufis
13. Spiritual Poverty in Sufism
14. Sufism III: Submission, Contentment, Absence, Presence, Intimacy, Awe, Tranquillity, Serenity, Fluctuation, Stability
15. Sufi Symbolism I: Parts of the Beloved's Body, Wine, Music, *Sama* and Convivial Gatherings
16. The Great Satan, 'Eblis'
17. Sufi Symbolism II: Love, Lover, Beloved,
18. Sufism IV: Repentance, Abstinence, Renunciation, Wariness, Humility, Humbleness, Sincerity, Constancy, Courtesy
19. Sufi Symbolism III: Religious Terminology
20. Dogs from the Sufi Point of View
21. Sufi Symbolism IV: The Natural World

SUFI WOMEN

Revised Second Edition

Dr. Javad Nurbakhsh

KHANIQAHI-NIMATULLAHI PUBLICATIONS
LONDON NEW YORK

Translated by Leonard Lewisohn
Edited by William Chittick
Designed by Jane Lewisohn

First published 1983
Second revised edition 1990

British Library Cataloguing in Publication Data
Nurbakhsh, Javad, 1927
Sufi Women, —Rev. Ed.
1.Sufism — Biographies — Collections
I. Title
297.40922
ISBN0-933546-42-4

Published by Khaniqahi-Nimatullahi Publications
41 Chepstow Place
London W2 4TS
England
Telephone: 071-229-0769

CONTENTS

LIST OF ILLUSTRATIONS

This book is dedicated to the pure soul of my mother, Mrs. Bibi Nurbakhsh. The verses below, taken from 'Aṭṭār's *Khosrow Nāmeh,* well express the relationship between her state and mine:

If ever I enjoyed the company of anyone,
it was the company of my mother.
But now she has gone.
Though Rāb'eh was a match for a hundred
spiritual warriors
she could not vie with that good woman,
my mother.
The ache in my soul will not let me describe
the grief that I now feel.
She was no mere woman, my mother,
but a spiritual man!
Mighty indeed were her night-long prayers,
and wonderful her midnight sighs, each
opening a way to God.
Detached from the world, she chose seclusion
from mankind,
a private corner, away from all creatures,
She turned her face to Thee, O guide,
knocking often on Thy door.
So open it

In the name of God, the Most Exalted and Sacred

A BRIEF HISTORY OF SUFISM

At first, Love's blaze
was not so scorching,
Yet whoever came along
fanned its flames
a little more.

Hājj Mollā Hādi Sabzevāri

The Appearance of Sufism

After the death of the Prophet of Islam, Muslims fell into disunity. A great number of different sects gradually made their appearance, out of which three main groups eventually emerged. One large group of Muslims was characterized by attention to Muslim tradition. The interest of this group in Islam was greatly influenced by Arab nationalism and by tribal parentage and kinship ties. The members of this group, which constituted the organizational nucleus of Islam, followed the Caliphs and came to be known as *sunni* (or adherents to Moḥammad's tradition).

Another group, impelled, as the saying goes, by the instinct of "in Autumn, seek the rose's scent from rosewater," became the followers of a number of the

Prophet's descendants, choosing in heart and soul to befriend certain members of the Prophet's family. This group of Muslims, a majority of whom were not Arab. came to be designated as *shi'ah* . Three main causes lay behind the inclination of these non-Arab peoples to become *Shi'ite.* First, many individuals of Iranian or Egyptian extraction tended towards *Shi'ism* as a result of their pre-Islamic cultural heritage. For example, among Iranian Zoroastrians, only the Magi's son traditionally had the right to succeed his father as priest, and anyone else's claim to this position was considered invalid. Similarly, the Egyptian belief in the divine right of the house of Pharaoh to rule made it unheard of for someone of non-royal blood to assume the ruling authority. In view of this heritage of religious and political beliefs, when these people converted to Islam they were naturally inclined to follow 'Ali and his progeny. Second, the negative response and opposition of 'Ali to the First Caliph during the initial days after the Prophet's death provided an historical basis for the *Shi'ite* sect to resist later Arab hegemony, thus resulting in the appearance of the first anti-Arab movement. Finally, these people were greatly influenced by the testimony of virtually all of the Prophet's companions that 'Ali was an incarnation of human virtue and perfection, and an incomparable treasury of Islamic knowledge. From the point of view of sanctity, he was considered to be the sole spiritual offspring of the Prophet of Islam and thus to be preferred over all others.

The final group that emerged from among the companions *(aṣḥāb)* and ascetics *(zohād)* of the Prophet's day consisted of those who remained aloof from all of these external concerns. Such people were not concerned with establishing themselves as a special sect, preferring instead to devote themselves solely to the preservation of the Islam of the Prophet's time. Their attention was focused not upon the social problems of the Islamic community, but upon the inner spiritual dimension of Islam, upon the worship of Allah and devotion to the One Reality *(al-ḥaqq).*

The first two groups mentioned above gradually grew further and further apart, falling into violent opposition and conflict. Their quarrels eventually culminated in the poisoning of Imam Ḥasan (the elder son of 'Ali and the second Shi'ite Imam) and the tragic martyrdom of Imam Ḥosain (the younger son of 'Ali). In the end, each group anathematized and persecuted the other, accusing it of infidelity and heresy.

In contrast to this divisiveness, the third group affirmed their allegiance to the 'Way of Moḥammad.' Since Moḥammad had cherished his companions, so too did they; since the Prophet had loved his family, they also loved them. At first, this group consisted solely of a handful of Moḥammad's companions. Later, however, it grew to include a few of the "followers" *(tāba'in)* or acquaintances of these Companions, who came to be designated as shaikhs (masters) or Friends of God *(awliyā-ye khodā).* In matters of faith, this group avoided being either exclusively Sunni or Shi'ite, preferring instead to foster the continuing existence of true Muslims. Indeed, instead of continuing to foster a cult of personality worship, they engaged themselves in devotion to God, wagering away all but Him in the gamble of love for God. The beliefs of this third group are illustrated in these verses of 'Aṭṭār:

Though you may know Abu Bakr and 'Ali,
my boy,
you are ignorant of the God of your reason and
soul.
Abandon all of these foolish events, and like
Rābe'ah,
day and night be a man of God!

When Shāh Ne'mato'llāh (d. 1437) was asked which school of Islam he followed, he composed the following verses:

"What is your faith?" they ask me,
O heedless ones, what faith should I have?
I possess a faith and rite
Far different than that of Shāfe'i and Abu Ḥanifa
They all follow the path of their own endeavor,
While I follow the way of my ancestor.[1]

Although some Sufis who were fond of 'Ali and his family came to be known as 'Shi'ite', and others were designated as 'Sunni' out of their respect for the Caliphs, in actuality the Sufis were neither, but rather true Muslims. It is this distinctively Sufi point of view that has caused both Sunni doctors of Islamic law and Shi'ite mullas throughout the ages to brand great Sufi masters and saints as heretics and issue orders to kill them.

---

[1] Shāh Ne'mato'llāh was a *sayyid* or direct descendant of the Prophet Moḥammad.

Koranic Verses Cited by Sufis

The Sufis have cited numerous verses of the Koran in support of their doctrine. Among them are the following:

"But those who struggle in Our cause, surely
We shall guide them in our ways."(XXIX:69)[1]

'Is it not time that the hearts of those who believe should be humbled to the remembrance of God and the Truth which He has sent Down, and that they should not be as those to whom the book was given afore time, and the term seemed over long to them, so that their hearts have become hard, and many of them are ungodly?" (LVII:16)

"And restrain thyself with those who call upon their lord at morning and evening, desiring His countenance, and let not thine eyes turn away from them, desiring the adornment of the present life and obey not himwhose heart We have made neglectful of Our remembrancesothat he follows his own lust, and his arrair has become all excess."(XVIII:28)

"The day whereon neither wealth nor sons shall profit, except for him who comes to God with a pure heart." (XXVI:88-9)

According to the Sufis, such verses refer to themselves.

---

[1]All Koranic quotations cited hereafter are from A.J. Arberry's The Koran Interpreted (Oxford University Press, 1983)

The Transformation of Sufism after the Seventh Century A.D.

In the early days of the development of Sufism, Sufis were primarily concerned with the keeping of vigils and asceticism *(zuhd).* The practice of keeping night vigil was one of the moral virtues for which the Prophet was highly respected, while asceticism arose from the Sufi's attempt to 'abandon the world.' The practice of asceticism basically consisted of silence, seclusion, fasting, and continual invocation of one of the Divine Names *(dhekr).*[1] Initially, the practice of *dhekr* encompassed not only the repetition of various Names of God and phrases (the most common one being *"la elāha ella' llāh,"* [there is no deity but Allah], but also ritual prayer *(namāz)*, recitation of Koranic verses *(qarā' at-e Qur'ān)*, and supplications *(ad' iya).*

The importance of these five basic practices of Sufism is expressed in the following Persian verse:

> *Continual rememberance of God,*
> *silence, wakefulness, fasting, and seclusion:*
> *With these five put into practice,*
> *the imperfect attain perfection.*

The exemplar of the practices of this stage in the evolution of Sufism was Ḥasan al-Basri (692-728). In his excessive abstinence and asceticism, he considered piety *(taqwā)* superior to both prayer *(ṣalāt)* and the ritual fasting of Islam *(ruzah).* Qoshayri relates that Ḥasan al-Basri once said, "A grain of true piety is better than a thousand bushels of prayer and fasting." A similar ascetic sentiment is expressed in the

[1]See the author's *In the Paradise of the Sufis,* Chapter II (ed).

following statement also attributed to him:

> O son of Adam, keep careful watch over your soul, for besides this soul you have no other. If your soul is saved, you will be saved; but if it is damned, you will be damned along with it. In the salvation of others, there is no benefit for you. All blessings besides Heaven are nothing, and all calamities other than Hellfire are slight.

Ḥātam Aṣam (d.852), a member of this same school, once declared:

> Whoever would embrace our faith must undergo four kinds of death: white death, black death, red death, and green death. The white death is hunger; the black death is the endurance of the torment of people; the red death is opposition to the lower soul; and the green death is the sewing of a robe out of patches.[1] (Solami, *Tabaqāt aṣ-ṣufiyyah).*

During this elementary stage, Sufis were full of devout hope for a heavenly reward in the hereafter and were terrified of hellfire, passing their lives in pursuit of perfect piety.

In the second stage of the development of Sufism, however, the elements of love *('eshq)* and loving kindness *(maḥabbat)* of God were added to the predominant asceticism. An emphasis on Divine Love gradually replaced the previous stress on the fear of God's chastisement. The sentiment usually voiced by

[1]In the early days of Sufism, Sufis were renowned as wearers of patched woolen cloaks known as *kherqa.* See Dr. Javad Nurbakhsh, *In The Tavern of Ruin,* Chapter 1.

Sufis of this period was that their worship of God was not out of fear of hellfire or hope for heaven, but rather out of the adoration and love that the Truth innately deserves. In support of this view, the following *ḥadith* was often cited: "This world is prohibited for people of the hereafter, and the hereafter is forbidden for the people of the world, and both worlds are forbidden to the people of God." Leaders among Sufis of this period included Rābe'ah, Bāyazid Bestāmi (d.874) and Shebli. With passionate intensity, Rābe'ah professed, "I swear by Your grandeur that I do not adore you out of longing for paradise or fear of hell, but for Your sublimity and magnificence alone I love and adore You."

In the ecstatic heights of her love of God, Rābe'ah even forgot to love His Prophet and curse Satan. Thus, "When asked do you love God?" she replied, "Yes." But when questioned as to whether she reviled Satan, she answered, "God's love leaves me no time to curse Satan." When Rābe'ah saw the Prophet in a dream, he asked her, "Do you love me?" She said: "O Prophet of God! Who is there who doesn't love you? But the love of God grants my heart no respite to remember the love of the creatures."

In a similar vein Shebli once said, "There are three sorts of death: for the love of this world, for the love of the next world, and for the love of God. Those who die in love of this world are hypocrites, those who die for love of the hereafter are ascetics, while those who die for the love of God are gnostics."

When Bāyazid Bestāmi was asked about asceticism, he replied, "Asceticism is no great thing. I was an ascetic for three days: on the first day I abstained from the world, on the second from the hereafter, and on the third from all else besides God."

In its third stage of development, both the ethical practice and the theory of Sufism expanded and achieved fruition. Among the great masters of ethical Sufism during this period we find Abu Sa'id Abo'l-Khair (d.1049) and Abo'l-Ḥasan Kharaqāni (d.1034). Among the formulators of Sufi mystical terminology, names such as Khāja Abdo'llāh Anṣāri (d.1089), Sanā'i (d.1131), and Farido'd-Din 'Aṭṭār (d.1221) must be mentioned. As for those Sufis who devoted themselves solely to the elaboration of the Way of Divine Love, Aḥmad Ghazzāli (d.1126), and Ruzbehān Baqli Shirāzi (d.1209) stand in the forefront.

In its fourth period of evolution, the speculative philosophy of Sufism, which was intimately bound up with the issue of "The Unity of Being" *(waḥdat al-wojud)*, entered an epoch of spectacular blossoming. The foremost exponent of this type of Sufism is Moḥyi'd-Din Ebn 'Arabi (d.1240).

The zenith of Sufism is generally considered to have occurred during the tenth, eleventh, twelfth and early part of the thirteenth century. From the latter part of the thirteenth century onwards, however, the mystic way gradually entered a descending arc, despite the occasional appearance of a few great masters such as Jalālo'd-Din Rumi (d.1273), Maḥmud Shabestari (d.1339), Fakhro'l-Din Erāqi (d.1289), and Shāh Ne'mato'llāh (d.1430). The majority of Sufis of this final period were charlatans, religious businessmen attired in Sufi robes, making extravagant but hollow claims. Sufism thus slowly lost its practical aspect and became increasingly abstract and theoretical. In these latter days, for instance, a perfect master was considered to be someone who knew and could interpret the works of Ebn 'Arabi.

The last half of the fifteenth century onwards saw even this speculative side of Sufism forgotten. The various masters of the Sufi way *(tariqat)* were of such low quality as to be unable to properly train disciples, thus distorting the true lineage of masterhood into a merely hereditary succession, confined to a particular family line. And so it has passed, until the present day and age, where it is clearly seen that Sufism is a sort of shopkeeping directed toward the acquisition of notoriety and wealth, in which all kinds of wares are on exhibition—except the goods of Sufism!

So it could be said: Sufism was at first a state of being, then mere words, while now neither the state nor the words remain.

Dr. Javad Nurbakhsh

PROLOGUE

Over and over again, people have asked this *faqir* the distinction, if any, between men and women in Sufism. The question often asked is whether or not there have been any women among the Sufis who attained the station of *Ensān-e-kāmel*, the Perfect Human Being.

In order to illumine the matter, and at the same time maintain reasonable brevity, we will discuss this problem from various perspectives.

Throughout the Koran, there are many instances in which God concurrently addresses both women and men believers. The significance of these exhortations is that, in terms of their Faith *(Imān)*, man and woman are equal. For instance, both are often mentioned side by side:

> *Men and women who have surrendered,*
> *believing men and believing women,*
> *obedient men and obedient women,*
> *truthful men and truthful women,*
> *enduring men and enduring women*
> *humble men and humble women,*
> *men and women who give in charity,*
> *men who fast and women who fast,*
> *men and women who guard their private parts.*
> *Men and women who remember God often*

for them God has prepared forgiveness
and a mighty wage.[1]

The following *ḥadith* is related of the Prophet Moḥammad: "God does not look at your forms." The essential implication of this tradition is that on the path of ascent toward the Truth, it is the heart's work that ultimately is weighed, not this corporeal form of flesh and blood.

Furthermore, all great Sufi masters have held the firm conviction that any woman who engages in the Path of Divine Love is not to be deemed "female" in the sense of being passive, but rather is to be judged solely by her humanity. The wide circulation of the following adage, popular for centuries among Sufis, testifies to this: "The seeker of God is masculine." *(ṭāleb al-mawlā modhakkar)* implying that, 'anyone who seeks God is a man-of-the Way."

Muḥyi'd-Din Ebn 'Arabi, in the seventy-third chapter of his monumental opus on Sufism, *Al- Fotuḥāt al-Makkiyya*, relates the following story:

> One of the masters was asked concerning the true number of the *abdāl*[2] existent in the world. 'There are altogether forty,' he answered .'Why not say: forty men?' they asked. 'Because there are women among them as well,' he replied.

Citing 'Abbāsa Ṭusi, in his *Memoirs of the Saints*, 'Aṭṭār has written, "When tomorrow, on Doomsday, the cry goes up: 'O men!' the first person to step forward will be Mary, the mother of Jesus."

[1]Koran, XXXIII: 35.
[2]Literally, meaning 'substitutes'. The Arabic term refers to one if the classes of *auliā'* or 'friends of God'.

Suffice it to say that women who seriously set foot on the path toward Reality are in exactly the same position as men who do so. Or, to express it somewhat differently, since in the Ocean of Divine Unity *(tawḥid)* neither 'I' nor 'you' exists, what meaning can 'man' or "woman" possibly have?

To give the reader a sense of the profound respect accorded to women in Sufism from the early days of Islam to the present day, we shall relate the biographies of a number of such women in this work, beginning with Rābe'ah, the most famous Sufi woman of early times, and ending with Hāyati, the most highly reputed of later times. It is hoped that this work may serve as a reminder of their struggles on the path of Divine Unity. In the words of the Arab poet:

If it is women we have sung of,
Well yes, woman excels man.
That the sun is feminine is no flaw,
Nor honor if the moon be masculine.[1]

---

[1]These lines belong to an anonymous Arab poet cited by Abdol-Rahmān Jāmi (d,1492) in the *Nafahāt al-ons*. In Arabic, the noun *Shams* (sun) is feminine and *Helāl* (moon) is masculine in gender (ed.).

RĀBE'AH AL-'ADAWIYA

Rābe'ah belongs to the elect company of Sufi women who have surpassed most of the contemporary Sufi masters of their time in wayfaring to God. If one wished to cite the names of some of the great Sufi saints from the early days of Islam to the present day, inevitably the name of Rābe'ah would be among them. That the excellence of Rābe'ah's piety *(taqwā)* gnosis *(ma'refat)*, and ascetic self-restraint *(zuhd)* have made her almost a symbol of saintliness among women Sufis suffices to illustrate her unparalleled status. Her perfection and the virtues of her soul *(fazā' el nafsāni)* evolved far beyond many of the later Sufi saints, making her renowned as the "Crown of Men" *(Tāj al rejal)*.

Farido'd-Din 'Aṭṭār's ecstatic praise of her in the *Conference of the Birds* echoes these sentiments:

No, she wasn't a single woman
But a hundred men over:
Robed in the quintessence of pain
From foot to face, immersed in the Truth,
Effaced in the radiance of God,
And liberated from all superfluous excess.

'Attār also praised Rābe'ah in his *Memoirs of the Saints:*

> That noble recluse who dwelled behind the cloisters of God's elect, a matron of sanctity beneath sincerity's veil, on fire with love, totally consumed with yearning, ardorously enraptured by God's proximity, that apostle of Mary's purity, acknowledged by all men was Rābe'ah al-Adawiya God's mercy rest upon her.

He has also written, "Both in terms of her spiritual transactions *(mo'āmalat)* and gnosis of God *(ma'refat)* Rābe'ah was unexcelled in her time and was accredited by all the great men of her age."

Rābe'ah's Early Years and Youth

Even though she is said to have belonged to the tribe of Al 'Atik, whose lineage is traced back to Noah, Rābe'ah was born into a family of poor circumstances. It is apparent that while her father and mother were destitute of this world's wares, Providence provided them with a nature capable of exercising great self denial and non-attachment to material wealth. When both of her parents died while she was still a young child, Rābe'ah was sold into slavery for an insignificant price and was forced to pass her youth in hard labour and destitution. 'Aṭṭār is better suited to tell of Rābe'ah's childhood:

> On the night Rābe'ah came into being it is related that there wasn't even a wrapping on hand to swaddle her with, nor a lamp, nor a drop of oil to

anoint her navel. Her father possessed three daughters and Rābe'ah was the fourth *(ar-Rābe'ah)*; thus, was she named: Rābe'ah. His wife told him: 'Go to the neighbor's house and ask them for a lamp and some oil.' Although Rābe'ah's father had already vowed not to ask anything of God's creatures, he arose, went next door and then returned telling his wife only, 'They are all asleep.' He then fell asleep, deeply grieved and heavy hearted, and Moḥammad the Prophet (may the Peace of God rest upon him) appeared to him in a dream, saying, 'Do not be grieved. You have been blessed with a daughter who will be a great saint; her intercession will be wished for by seventy thousand of my community.'

The Prophet then commanded him further, 'Tomorrow send a letter to 'Isa Rādān, Amir of Basra, reminding him, by this sign, that every night he is wont to offer one hundred benedictions to me, and on Friday night, four hundred. But this Friday he has neglected me so tell him that, as a penance, he must give you a hundred dinars.'

Waking at dawn, Rābe'ah's father, in tears, noted his dream down in a letter, went to the court of 'Isā Rādān, and handed it to a chamberlain to give to the Amir. After perusing the letter, 'Isā Rādān commanded, 'Ten thousand dinars should be distributed to the poor as a thanksgiving offering since the Prophet deigned to mention me.' Ordering that four hundred dinars be given to Rābe'ah's father, he commented, 'Though I wish that such a person should come to me, rather I will come and sweep the dust from his doorstep with my beard. For God's sake though, whenever he is in need, please let me know.' And so Rābe'āh's father brought home the gold and spent it.

After Rābe'ah's parents passed away, a severe famine arose in Basra, and all her sisters scattered while she fell into the hands of a cruel man who auctioned her off as a slave for a few dirhams. When a stranger approached her in the street one day, she became frightened and tried to flee but fell in the dust, breaking her wrist. Prostrating herself in the mud, she confessed, 'O God, I am a stranger, without father or mother; I have been sold in bondage, and now my wrist is broken. But despite all this, I am not distressed about anything that has befallen me. I only wish you to be content, so that I might know if I have gained your satisfaction or not.' She then heard an unseen voice tell her, 'Do not mourn, for in the hereafter you will reach such a rank that even those nearest to God in heaven will be proud of your station.'

Rābe'ah then turned to her master's house and began to fast constantly, praying through each night. During the day she remained on her feet, occupied with her household chores. One night her master awoke and, hearing a cry, stared over to see Rābe'ah awake with her forehead bowed to the floor in supplication. 'O God,' she confessed, 'You are aware that the sole longing of my heart is to be totally surrendered to your command. The very light of my eyes is service to Your court. If it were up to me, I would never cease serving you, even for an hour. Yet you have caused me to be subject to a creature. For this, I come late to your service.'

After hearing this speech, her master rose and

pondered to himself, 'Such a woman cannot be confined to slavery.' In the morning he summoned Rābe'ah and set her free, remarking, 'If you remain with us, we shall all serve you; if you do not wish this to happen, go where you will.' Rābe'ah asked for her leave and departed. She subsequently devoted herself to various works of piety. Within every twenty-four hour period, she was said to perform a thousand *rak'ats* of the ritual prayer. One report relates that she followed the profession of a flute player for a while. Then she repented and lived homeless among the ruins. Finally, she made a cell of seclusion for herself and occupied herself soley with acts of devotion. In the end, she set out on the pilgrimage to Mecca and retired to the desert.

Rābe'ah and marriage

It seems quite doubtful that Rābe'ah ever married. Her manner of rejecting the marriage propsal of Moḥammad Ebn Solaimān Hāshemi, Governor of Basra, seems to testify to this. "Where you to bequeath me all your wealth," she replied to his offer, "it would be impossible for me to turn from God to you for even the blink of an eye."

To others who inquired why she never married, Rābe'ah's repeated reply was, "The marriage bond concerns a 'being' but where is 'being' to be found (in me)? I do not belong to myself. I am His possession."

If she indeed did marry, which appears rather improbable, it was only for a short time in her early life. In any case all that has been written concerning Rābe'ah's marriage with 'Abdo'l-Wāhed Ebn Zaid undoubtedly concerns Rābe'ah Demashqi, who will be spoken of later on in this book. Many authorities have often mistaken the two saints for each other.

Rābe'ah's Devout Way of Life

Rābe'ah's nights were occupied in sleepless vigilance, and her days in the worship of God. It is said that she was deeply absorbed in grief and wept exceedingly.

The following account, attributed to Rābe'ah by 'Abda Bent Abi Showāl, a lady devoted to Rābe'ah's service, is related in the *Ṣefat al-ṣafwat* of Ebn al-Jawzi:

> Rābe'ah used to pray all night, only then permitting herself to doze lightly before dawn until the shadow of daybreak tinted the horizon. Then she would rise and say, possessed by deep fear, 'O soul, how long shall you go on with this sleeping and waking? The time is near when you will sleep so much that only the trumpet call of the Resurrection will summon you awake.' This was her way of life until she died, extremely eager to maintain the night vigil unless some task arose that kept her from it.

In the same work, Ebn Jawzi narrates 'Abdo'llāh ebn 'Isā's account of his meeting with Rābe'ah:

> When I entered Rābe'ah's house, I percieved her face radiant with a brilliant sheen from her constant crying. A man sat near her, reciting a verse from the Koran concerning Hellfire, whereupon she burst out in tears, then she cried

out and fainted.

Another time she was seated on a mat of woven reeds when we entered her presence. A man near to her was lecturing on some matter while her tears poured like rain onto the torn reed-mat. In sudden agitation she cried out. Then we all arose and took our leave.

Abdo'r-Ra'uf Monāwi in the *Ṭabaqāt al-auliyā' (Classes of the Saints)* has also noted that Rābe'ah was "extremely fearful."

Ḥasan al-Basri gives the following account of her nature:

> In her whole house I saw only a pitcher with a chip on its spout, which she used to perform ablutions as well as drink water, a brick which she used as a pillow, and a mat of woven reeds on which she prayed. Besides this, there was nothing else. Whatever people bestowed on her she rejected, saying, 'I have no need of the world.'

Monāwi writes in the *Ṭabaqāt al-auliyā'* that "Rābe'ah felt so ashamed before God that for forty years she never raised her head to heaven."

Rābe'ah's Old Age

Ebn Jawzi, in the *Ṣefat al-ṣāfwat,* relates the following story from Moḥammad Ebn 'Amr:

> When I entered Rābe'ah's presence, she was an aged woman of eighty years, brittle as dried skin. It seemed that if you touched her she would

crumble to pieces. In her house I saw only a split reed-mat and a clothes stand of Persian reed, which was two meters wide. The covering of her house was of plain branches. There was also a water pitcher and a bit of sheep's wool beside her bed and place of prayer. Next to these was a reed-mat on which she had placed her shroud. Whenever death was mentioned, she would tremble, visibly possessed by shivering. It is related that a pool of water from her tears lay gathered beside the place where she prostrated during prayers.

In his *Memoirs of the Saints,* 'Aṭṭār writes of Rābe'ah's spiritual magnanimity:

> Concerning Rābe'ah's death, great Sufi masters all averred: 'Rābe'ah came into the world and went unto the hereafter; she never exalted or vaunted herself before God, never wanted anything, never saying, 'Do so much for me' or 'Provide me with this.'

Rābe'ah's Death

There is no unanimity among scholars concerning the date of Rābe'ah's death. Various historians offer differing accounts. The date 135/753 is cited by Ebn Jawzi in the *Shodhur al-'oqud,* Abu'l-Maḥāsen Taghriberdi in the *Al-Nojum al-zāhera,* Mortaḍhā Zobaydi in the *Itteḥāf al-sādat al amottaqin,* Ebn al-Molqan in the *Tabaqāt al-'āuliya,* and Ebn 'Emād Ḥanbali in the *Shadharāt al-dhahab.*

According to Dhahabi and Abdur-Ra'uf Monāwi in the *Tabaqāt al-auliyā',* Rābe'ah passed away in 180/

796 Ebn Khallekān and Ebn Shāker al Kotobi in their biographical histories, and 'Emād al-Din Abo'l-Fadā' Esmā'il Ebn 'Omar Ebn Kathir al-Qoraishi al-Demashqi (d.1373) in his book *al-Bedāyah wa'l-nahāya*, put her death date as 185/801 the later date is also cited for Rābe'ah's death by Dārā Shokuh in the *Safinat al-auliyā'*.

A list of the death dates of various personages who are said to have been acquainted with Rābe'ah or to have existed during her lifetime is as follows.

"Ṣāleḥ Mari (d. 172-76 / 788-792)
'Abd al-Wāḥed Ebn Zayd of Basra (d. 177/ 793)
Moḥammad Ebn Solaimān Hāshemi (governor of Basra) (d. 170/ 789)
Rabāḥ Ebn 'Amr al-Qaysi (d. 180-95 / 796-810)
Sofyān Thawri (d. 161/ 778)

Considering the above dates, it seems probable, for three reasons, that Rābe'ah passed away sometime between 180-85/796-801. First of all, Moḥammad Ebn Solaimān al-Hāshemi (who once sought Rābe'ah's hand) was the Abbasid governor of Basra from 145/ 762 to 170/787 when he died. Second of all, Rabāḥ al-Qaysi, a close associate of Rābe'ah, passed away in 180/797 or 185/801 and thirdly, Sofyān Thawri's arrival in Basra was subsequent to the year 155/772. One further point remains to be clarified, that is to saythe so-called encounter between Rābe'ah and Ḥasan al-Basri is unanimously acknowledged as 110/728. Thus, unless we were to posit the existence of another Ḥasan al-Basri, it may be positively stated that the two actually never met.

On the subject of Rābe'ah's place of burial, some authorities seem to have confused the grave of Rābe'ah of Syria with that of Rābe'ah al-'Adawiya of Basra. Rābe'ah's grave is sometimes said to be at the top of the Mount of Olives in Jerusalem. This, however, is incorrect. Rābe'ah al-'Adawiya's sepulchre is actually at Basra.

Anecdotes and Adages of Rābe'ah [1]

1. After Rābe'ah set out for Mecca, she was forced to stay in the desert for a few days ."Oh God," she cried out, "my heart is heavy with sorrow. Where am I going to? I am but a handful of dirt, and your house is only a stone. You are my sole desire."

Without mediation, God addressed her heart, saying, "You are approaching the blood of the eighteen thousand worlds. If I were to manifest Myself to the Universe as I am, all would be scattered. Do you wish to cause such destruction? Do you not know what happened when Moses requested a vision of Me? I scattered but a few atoms of Theophany on the peak of Mt. Sinai and it was shattered into forty pieces." (Koran VII:143)

2. They say that when Rābe'ah was performing the pilgrimage to Mecca through the desert, she saw the Ka'ba itself coming out to receive her. "I want the Lord of the house," she cried. "What can I do with this Ka'ba? I pay no attention to the Ka'ba and enjoy not it's beauty. My only desire is to encounter Him who

[1]The following stories, unless otherwise indicated, are all translated from the *Tadhkerat al-auliyā' Memoirs of the Saints* by Farido'd-Din Aṭṭār (d.1221) (ed.).

said, 'Whosoever approaches Me by a span, I will approach him by a cubit.'[1] What benefit can I recieve from seeing the Ka'ba?"

3. Rābe'ah owned only a donkey to transport her luggage when she set out in the desert on pilgrimage to Mecca. In the middle of the desert, her donkey died. When her fellow travellers offered to bear her bags, she replied, "You go on. Not by trusting you have I come thus far." The caravan then continued on, leaving her there, "O God, is this the way Monarchs behave with helpless women?" Rābe'ah cried. "You invited me to Your dwelling, then on the way make my donkey die, leaving me stranded in the heat of the desert!" Instantly, her donkey revived and arose. She laid her luggage on it and proceeded on her way.

4. It is related that Ebrāhim Adham (d.782) spent fourteen years traversing the desert until he arrived at the Ka'ba. "Others walk on foot to Mecca," he remarked, "while I tread on my eyes." His habit was to make two genuflections of ritual prayer for every one step forward. On attaining to Mecca, however, the Ka'ba had disappeared. "What has happened?" he asked, rubbing his eyes, "perhaps I've become dim-sighted."

"Your vision is fine," a mysterious voice informed him. "Only the Ka'ba went to recieve a lady on her way here."

"Who can she be?" he cried aghast with envy. Then he beheld Rābe'ah hobbling along the way, cane in

---

[1]The full version of this *ḥadith qodsi* (sacred Prophetic tradition) is to be found in the author's work, *Traditions of the Prophet*, volume I, p. 2.

hand. The Ka'ba returned to its place. "O Rābe'ah, what is this riot and commotion you have created in the world?" Ebrāhim demanded.

Rābe'ah retorted, "It is you who are the real cause of commotion in the world, having waivered fourteen years in crossing the desert to reach God's Shrine"

"Of course," he pleaded, " for fourteen years I was preoccupied in ritual prayer *(namāz)* on my journey."

"Through ritual prayer you journeyed," Rābe'ah replied, "whereas I made my way by means of desperate spiritual supplication and need *(niyāz).*" Rābe'ah then completed the pilgrimage and wept in grief, saying "O God! You have given us assurances of Your approbation and good will, both for our pilgrimage and for our adversity. If my pilgrimage is unacceptable now (which itself is adversity), where is Your reward for the adversity I have endured?" She then returned to Basra until the next year. "If last year," she commented, "the Ka'ba came out to meet me, this year I shall go to greet the Ka'ba"

5. According to Shaikh Fārmadi,[1] Rābe'ah crawled on her side for seven years until she reached Mt. Arafat.[2] Once there, an unseen voice censured her, "You imposter, what is all this 'quest' you are preoccupied with? If you desire Me, then I will show one flash of My Glory and consume you." Rābe'ah then entreated: "O Lord of Majesty, Rābe'ah lacks such a capacity, but

[1]Abu 'Ali Faḏhl Ebn Moḥammad Fārmadi was a Sufi master who was born in 1084 in the village of Fārmad, a suburb of Tus, a city in Khorāsan in Northeastern Iran. Shaikh Yāfe'i in his book *Motawaffiyāt (Obituaries)* mentions the date of his death as 1084 (ed).

[2]Portions of this translation are adapted from: M. Smith, *Rābi'ah the Mystic, and Her Fellow Saints in Islam*, p. 75.

I yearn for the essence of spiritual poverty *(faqr)*." The voice responded, "O Rābe'ah, Poverty is the scourge of Our Wrath, which we have placed on the Saints' path. When less than a hair's width remains between them and Our Union, We turn their affairs topsy-turvy and cast them into bereavement. Yet you are still enthralled by seventy thousand veils of your own day and age. Only when you emerge from beneath these veils and step firmly upon the Way will you be worthy to profess that poverty. If not, then look up." As she lifted her eyes, she beheld an ocean of blood, suspended in midair.

The same invisible voice recounted, "Those lovers who perished in their search before attaining to the first way-station of Union with Us — this ocean is the blood of their hearts. In neither world and in no stage of the Way is any name or indication to be found of them."

"O Almighty Lord, allow me to view but a token of the grace they have attained," Rābe'ah beseeched. Instantaneously, Rābe'ah began to menstruate.[1] "The primary stage of their Way," the voice answered, is that they crawl on their sides for seven years to render homage to an earthen clod.[2] As they near this selfsame clod, however, We deny them access to their goal, by reason of themselves." Rābe'ah became inflamed upon hearing this. "Lord," she cried, "You neither grant me entry into Your mansion nor pernit me to rest in my own house in Basra. Either let me into Your House in Mecca or leave me home in Basra. Once, so deep was my yearning for You, that I wouldn't even presume to

[1]During menstruation, women are prohibited from saying ritual prayers, reading the Korān, entering a mosque, etc (ed)
[2]*I.e.*, the Ka'ba (ed)

approach Your house. Now I do not even merit entrance." So saying, Rābe'ah turned back to Basra and remained secluded in her home.

'Aṭṭār has rendered the above account in verse in *The Conference of the Birds (Manṭeq at-Ṭayr):*

Rābe'ah, Crown of Men
For seven years prone
On her belly crept to the Ka'ba
Then paused by the Sacred Mosque
To heave a sigh of relief,
A pilgrim fulfilled.
Then as she tried to enter
Was outcast by the pretext of sex,
Exposed by "women's alibi."
"O God Omnipotent," she cried
"For seven years, abased and prone,
Haven't I suffered? Haven't I sought You?
If this is the game today,
To ambush me with briars so sharp,
— I will go away.
Either grant me rest alone at home
Or open my passage
Into the Ka'ba's sanctuary!"
Unless you are ravished in loves' fervor
Like Rābe'ah, what gnosis
Will you posses of this experience?
Wander about as you will
Idly in this sea of fancy—
And let the waves of sentient success
And failure sway and sweep you
Sometimes they will entreat you
"Step up in the Ka'ba!"
Sometimes offer you a job inside a monastery
But if you elevate your vision
Beyond this maelstorm of confusion

Each Breath will reinspire
Another, newer, Heart-consciousness.
If you remain in this eddy of misery,
Like grain under the millstone, you will be split
In spirit— you will be ground, head to foot.
You will never understand the measure
Of Time: a fly will veil you from eternity,
And never an instant will you imbue
A scent of the heart's unity.
For not even an instant will you catch
The scent of "gathering": a mere fly
Will disturb your "moment".

6. Two shaikhs once came to pay their respects to Rābe'ah. Both happened to be hungry, and they reflected, "Whatever she offers us will assuredly be permitted by Islamic law." They seated themselves and she set two loaves of bread before them. At that moment, a beggar presented himself, asking for alms and Rābe'ah gave him both loaves. Though both men were astounded at her behaviour, they made no objections. A maidservant then entered Rābe'ah's cottage with an armful of warm bread. "My mistress," she explained, "has sent these for you." Rābe'ah took them; there were eighteen loaves, "There must be some error," she remarked. "Please take them back to your mistress." Though the girl protested, Rābe'ah insisted they be returned. When the maidservant brought the loaves back to her mistress and recounted the story, the lady supplemented her gift by two additional loaves. This time when the girl brought the loaves to Rābe'ah, the saint acknowledged the gift of twenty loaves. Rābe'ah laid the loaves before her guests and, though surprised, they enjoyed the meal.

Afterwards, they ventured to ask Rābe'ah the mystery of the events they had witnessed. "As you entered," said Rābe'ah, "I saw you both were hungry, but I felt it wouldn't be becoming to offer such notables as yourselves so meagre a fare as two loaves. Therefore, I bestowed them on the begger, entreating, "O God, you have promised to repay our charity tenfold. This is beyond doubt. I have offered You two loaves; grant me a tenfold return then." When the maidservant brought only eighteen, I saw that a mistake had occurred, or else they had been incorrectly delivered to me. I returned them until the proper amount I had petitioned for arrived."

7. One night, preoccupied with prayers in her chamber, sleep overcame Rābe'ah. When a blade of straw entered her eye, so intense was her yearning and so extreme was her contrition that she remained unconscious of any injury.

8. Another night a thief entered her cell and seized her *chaddur.*[1] As he tried to make off with it, he found the way barred to him. He laid the *chaddur* aside and immediately the door opened.

When he again picked up the *chaddur* however, he discovered that the passage was again closed. He experienced this seven times until, from a nook of Rābe'ah's cell, a mysterious voice addressed him, "She has entrusted herself to Us all these years. Since even the Devil is afraid here, how can a thief like you even dare to circle her *chaddur*? Begone, you rogue, because if one friend falls asleep, the other Friend is

[1]A veil worn from head to foot in some Muslim countries (ed.).

vigilant and awake."[1]

According to one exegesis, this story is a demonstration of the verity of the Koranic verse, "Over each person stands a guardian assigned; behind his back, before his face, to watch over him, by God's will." (XI:I3)

9. Rābe'ah's maidservant was preparing a stew one day since neither she nor Rābe'ah had eaten for some time. Finding herself in need of onions, she proposed to her mistress to ask the neighbors. "Forty years now," Rābe'ah replied, "have passed since I vowed to God, the Majestic and Transcendent, never to request anything from anyone but Him. Forego the onions." Suddenly a bird swooped from the skies and cast a few perfectly peeled onions into the frying pan. "There still might be deceit *(makr)*[2] in this operation," Rābe'ah remarked. Setting aside the entire stew, she dined on dry bread.[3]

10. One day Rābe'ah had gone to the mountains, and hordes of wild beasts, goats and gazelles thronged about her. When Ḥasan al-Basri suddenly appeared on the scene, and they all scattered in fright. Inwardly perturbed by this event, Ḥasan entreated Rābe'ah, "Why did they make friends with you but flee from me?"

---

[1]A poetic version of this story is provided by 'Aṭṭār in his *Moṣibat Nāmah. (The Book of Afflictions)* (ed.).

[2]This word is used in the Korān in connection with Satanic temptations and trials, which is probably its meaning here (ed.).

[3]The author of the *Montakhab Rawnaq al-majāles* cites this story by word of 'Abdo'l-Wāḥed ebn Zayd.

"What was your meal today?" Rābe'ah asked in return. "A mere broth," said Ḥasan.

"Well, you eat of their fat. Why shouldn't they be in fear of you?"[1]

11. On one occasion, Rābe'ah happened to be strolling in the alleyway beside Ḥasan al-Basri's residence. Ḥasan was on top of the roof, weeping abundantly, when a few drops struck Rābe'ah. "What's this?" she mused. Deducing it to be Ḥasan's teardrops, she called out, "O Ḥasan, if these are the sobs of your ego's foolishness, control yourself until such a sea gathers within you that if you seek the heart, you will not find it except 'in the keeping of an Emperor Omnipotent.' (Koran: LIV:55)

Though these words were difficult for Ḥasan, he held his peace. A few days later, while strolling by the side of the Euphrates, Ḥasan saw Rābe'ah. After heaving his prayer mat out on the river's surface, he beckoned her, "Come! Let us say two *ra'kat* of prayer out here."

"O master," was Rābe'ah's rebuttal, "in this world's market you have displayed the character of the inhabitants of the hereafter. Try rather to advertise in such a way that others will be impotent to imitate you." Unfurling her prayer mat in midair, Rābe'ah challenged Ḥasan, saying, " Ascend upon here, where you'll be concealed from observation of mankind." Seeking to console Ḥasan's wounded feelings, she added, "Fishes also do what you did, while what I do is but a mosquito's performance. Real work transcends both."

---

[1]'Aṭṭār renders this tale in verse in his *Book of Divinity (Elāhi Nāmah)* (ed).

12. "I spent a day and a night with Rābe'ah discussing the *ṭariqat* and the *ḥaqiqat*," relates Ḥasan al-Basri, "yet never did it occur to either Rābe'ah or myself that one of us was female and the other male. But I discovered myself to be destitute when I left her, while she, I saw, was in her dedication utterly pure *(mokhleṣ)*."

13. Ḥasan and some friends paid Rābe'ah a visit late one evening. Rābe'ah owned no lamp, but since the group thought one was needed, Rābe'ah blew lightly on her fingers, which remained aflame, acting as a lantern until daybreak. If anyone makes objections to this, I would answer, " It is the same as the white hand of Moses." "But he was a Prophet," perhaps such a person will respond. To which I say, "Likewise followers of a Prophet imbue a bit of his charismatic blessing *(karāmāt)*. The Divine endowment of the Prophet *(nabi)* consists of miracles *(mo'jezah)*, whereas the saint *(wali)* is blessed by virtue of obedience to a Prophet with [similar] charismatic powers *(karāmāt)*.[1] In the words of the Prophet, "Whosoever repudiates a penny's worth of the unlawful has attained one degree of Prophethood," He has also said, "A true dream is a fortieth part of Prophecy."

14. Rābe'ah, on one occasion, sent three things to Ḥasan: a bit of wax, a needle, and a hair. "Light the world," she exhorted him, "though like wax you burn yourself. And like a needle, be always engaged in the spiritual work, while outwardly barren. Upon

[1]In traditional Islamic terminology, *mo'jezah* is considered to be a form of miraculous ability reserved for Prophets, while similar acts performed by saints are called *karāmāt* (ed.).

acquisition of these virtues, then become a hair (do not see yourself) so that your work will not be wasted."

15. Ḥasan once asked Rābe'ah whether she would like to take a husband. She replied, "The marriage contract is bound to a 'being.' But here 'being' is absent. Of myself I am unaware; alone through Him I am, and under the shadow of His will I exist. My husband must be sought from Him."

"How did you attain to this station?" questioned Ḥasan."

"Through losing all my attainment in Him." she replied.

"How do you know Him, then?" Ḥasan inquired.

"You know 'how'," she answered. " I know without 'how'. "

16. Ḥasan entered Rābe'ah's convent one day and engaged her in a conversation about "knowledge that could not be acquired through either learning or listening." He asked her to describe the knowledge that had entered her heart without any creature's mediation. She replied, "I spun a few spools of yarn to sell for food and earned two dirhams. In each hand I placed a dirham; I feared to put both together in one hand—that their wealth, when gathered, might waylay me. This was my spiritual realization for today."[1]

[1] 'Aṭṭār included a poetic version of this story in *The Conference of the Birds.* (ed.).

17. Rābe'ah was told that Ḥasan al-Basri had said, "If in paradise, the vision of the Truth even for a moment is withheld from me, I will cry and mourn so much that all the inhabitants of heaven will have compassion for me."

"Fine words," remarked Rābe'ah, "but when one fails to invoke God for one breath in this world and such a state of weeping, grief and misery appears, this is a sign that in the hereafter such will also be one's state. Otherwise, it is not so."

18. People asked Rābe'ah, "Why do you not marry?" She replied, "I have been left bewildered by worry over three things. If you free me from having to worry about them, I will marry. First of all, at the moment of death, shall my faith be sufficient to bring me to salvation? Second, will the book of my deeds be given to me in my left or right hand?[1] Third, upon that hour when a party of people are called forth on the left hand to Hell, and another group from the right hand are summoned to Heaven, which company will I belong to?"

"Of this, we are ignorant," they informed her. "With this anxiety that afflicts me then," she replied, "how can I ever marry?"

Shaikh Sho'aib ebn 'Abdo'l-'Aziz al-Ḥorayfaysh in his book *al-Rowḍh al-Fā'iq,* has added a fourth question to 'Aṭṭār's account of this story: "When I am interrogated in the grave by the two angels of death, Monkar and Nakir, shall I be able to answer their questions or not?"

---

[1] The records of the deeds of the righteous, according to the Koran, are given to them in their right hands on the Judgement Day, whereas evil-doers receive theirs in their left hands.

19. Rābe'ah once saw a man with a bandage bound around his head. "What's this bandage you've tied about yourself?" Rābe'ah asked.

"I have a headache," he responded.

"What's your age?" Rābe'ah asked.

"Thirty," he answered.

"Have you had good health, overall, throughout your life, or pain and infirmity?" Rābe'ah asked.

"Good health, mostly," he answered.

"You have never bound a bandage about yourself to express your gratitude to God for this excellent health, yet now for the sake of a minor headache you wind a bandage of complaint around your head!"

20. Rābe'ah once handed someone four dirhams and asked him to buy her a blanket.

"Would you prefer black or white?" the person asked.

Taking the money back and throwing it into the Tigris, Rābe'ah said, "The blanket has not yet been bought and its color has already become a cause of discord."

21. One fine spring day, Rābe'ah retired into seclusion in her hermitage, not intending to emerge. Then her servant-girl entreated, "Oh mistress, come out and behold the works of the Creator."

"Rather, you come in," answered the saint, "and view the Creator Himself. Contemplation of Him keeps me from beholding His creation."[1]

[1]A poetic version of this story is included in 'Aṭṭār's *Book of Adversities.* (ed.)

22. Once a party came to Rābe'ah and observed that she sliced meat with her teeth. "Have you no knife?" they inquired.

"I fear separation so much," replied Rābe'ah, "that I never possessed a knife."

23. Once Rābe'ah maintained a fast for a week. Smitten with terrible hunger pangs on the eighth evening, her lower soul (*nafs)* began to complain. "How much longer shall you subject me to torment?" Suddenly, she heard a knock on her door. Rābe'ah opened it to find a lady with a kettle of food as charity. Rābe'ah accepted the offering and went to fetch a candle. Returning, she saw the cat had upset the vessel. "I'll break my fast with water," she mused and went in search of a pitcher. Just then the candle expired. When she tried to quench her thirst in the dark, the pitcher's handle cracked and crashed to the ground. She sighed in such a way that it seemed the house would catch afire. "O Lord," she exclaimed in bewilderment, "what is all this You are doing to make me so helpless?"

"Were you only to so wish it," a mysterious voice informed her, "all worldly advantages would be ceded to you, yet Our love's grief, in consequence, We would remove from your heart. Love's grief and worldly benefits cannot be accumulated together at the same time in one heart, dear Rābe'ah. You have intentions and We have intentions as well. Our intention and your intention cannot be united together in one heart."

After hearing these words, Rābe'ah recalled, "I severed my heart so utterly from this world and so completely restrained my desires that for the last thirty years I have made each prayer as if it were the last I would ever perform. I have so absolutely broken my ties with people that when each day breaks, fearing that people will distract and engage my heart, I pray, 'Lord engage me solely with Yourself so none shall distract me from You'."

A poetic version of this tale exists in 'Aṭṭār's *Book of Divinity (Elahi nāmeh)*:

Be as Rābe'ah: a true spiritual princess,
Headmistress of our mystic Way's
many waystations.
She whose sole toil was unceasing prayer;
Fasting the night-long awake, never despairing,
Always on foot, dawn to dusk,
Until lassitude and fatigue toppled her,
Hunger's debility seized her limbs,
Brought by weariness to her last legs.

The same moment she nearly swooned
A lady appeared, presenting a kettle:
Fare for breaking fast.
Anxious, aggrieved, and stranded in the dark
Rābe'ah rose in search
Of a lamp to light her meal.
Returning, she found a cat had knocked
Down the kettle of charity,
So she sought a pitcher
To quench her fast instead
With limpid water.
Returning, the wick died —
Rābe'ah's mind lost all bearings,
And like a candle expired in despair.
Wearied and lost in the darkness,
Vanquished by thirst, with the vase to her lip,

The pitcher crashed and smashed to the earth —
Her insides were set afire.

Dazed, her sighs suspired
Her heart flaming, stirring a universe afire,
She cried and cried, "Lord
From me, from one so miserable,
What is your desire?
You've consumed me, caught me in distraction,
Dissipated my soul so much in unconsciousness,
Through how much more blood must I wade?"

"Your every ambition we'll grant you
In heaven and earth, from Fish to Moon"
Came the Beloved's address,
"Yes, yet the grief of endless years
Forever from your heart will disappear,
Consider this carefully, Rābe'ah,
Within a single heart God's grief
Along side worldly deceit, cannot exist
Were a hundred years' span spread by."

To no one is Divinity's grief given for free.
If God's lovesickness is your wish,
Make your profession
Incessant abandonment of this world,
For until you creach this abandonment,
You are veiled
From the vision of everything otherworldly.

24. It is related that Rābe'ah engaged in constant crying and lamentation. People would say to her, "Outwardly, this weeping seems senseless, why should you weep?" She would reply, "Deep within my breast lies the reason for my bereavement and pain. This

malady no doctor can remedy. The sole cure of this pain is Union with the Friend, and by this mourning I hope that perhaps hereafter I will reach what I seek. Though I was not originally conceived in that Divine Grief, I attempt to simulate the state of those who are truly afflicted with Divine Love, that I may be deemed no less than they."

25. A company of famous men once paid Rābe'ah a visit. She demanded of them, "Why do you worship God?"

"Seven levels of Hell exist," one replied, "through which everyone must descend in shock and terror."

Another said, "There are sublime abodes of beauty in paradise where peace and tranquility are guaranteed."

Rābe'ah responded, "Only a bad slave is devoted to his master out of fear of chastisement or desire for reward."

"Then what is the cause of your worship of God?" they inquired. "Have you no covetousness?"

"The neighbor first, then his house," replied Rābe'ah quoting an Arabic proverb. "Is it not sufficient that we are commanded to worship Him? Should we rather cease to adore Him were Heaven and Hell assumed non-existent? Should He not rather be adored beyond all mediation?"

26. A notable man once went to visit Rābe'ah. Observing her tattered clothes, he said, "There are quite a few people I know who would regard you with a charitable eye, if you would only permit it."

"It really embarrasses me," Rābe'ah confessed, "to

ask anything of this world from anyone who possesses it only temporarily."

"Look!" he exclaimed, "at this weak woman's exalted aspiration: she deplores wasting time asking for alms!"

27. In an attempt to test Rābe'ah's piety, a group of people unexpectedly dropped in on her. "Every single virtue," they argued, "has been showered on the heads of men. The Girdle of Noble Beneficence is bound only about men's waists, while the Crown of Chivalry rests solely on men's heads. No woman has ever been inspired by Prophecy. So what is all your vaunting?"

"Everything you have said is true," replied Rābe'ah with equanimity. "But vanity, egotism, selfish conceit, and 'I am your Lord Most High'[1] have never risen from a woman's bosom, nor has any woman ever been a pederast."

28. One day Rābe'ah fell sick. When asked about the reason for her illness, she said, "At dawn my heart inclined fondly toward paradise. By way of this malady, I have been reproved by the Friend. This is the cause of my sickness."

This same anecdote is related in a slightly different form in the *Kholāsa-ye sharḥ-e ta'arrof:*

> Once a party of people paid Rābe'ah a visit to offer their condolence during one of her bouts of sickness and weeping. When they asked after her health, she replied, 'All I know, I swear to God, is that recently Heaven was revealed to me, and I felt a slight inclination of heart towards it. I

[1]The claim of Pharoah (ed.).

reckon that the All-Mighty's jealousy has chastised me through this sickness. It is a sort of Divine reproof.'

29. Ḥasan al-Basri set out to pay his respects to Rābe'ah. "There was a well-to-do notable of Basra whom I saw," he related, "kneeling at the portal of her hermitage in tears, clutching a purse of gold in his hand.

"Sire, why do you weep?" I inquired of him.

"For the sake of this blessed ascetic, this holy saint of our age," he replied. "For without the sanctity of her presence all people would perish. I've brought a little insignificant something for her welfare; intercede for me and perhaps she will accept it."

"I entered Rābe'ah's chamber and relayed the message. Out of the corner of her eye, Rābe'ah shot me a glance and observed, 'Since God does not expropriate the daily sustenance of one who curses Him, how then should He not provide for one whose soul is seething with His Love? I have totally turned my back on all creatures, ever since my very first acquaintance with Him. And if I am not sure whether someone's property is lawful, how should I accept it? Using the Sultan's lamp one time, I patched a blouse, but then my heart contracted and remained closed and tight until I had undone every stitch. Ask the gentleman not to cause my heart further constriction.' "

30. "I went with Sofyān Thawri," (d.778) relates 'Abdo'l Wāḥed Ebn 'Amer, "to pay Rābe'ah a visit while she was sick. Her presence, however, so overwhelmed us with awe that both of us were struck dumb."

'Say something,' I urged Sofyān.

'Why don't you ask God to alleviate your pain?' he asked her.

'He Himself wills that I suffer, isn't that obvious to you?' she rejoined.

'Yes,' I affirmed.

'Still despite your knowledge,' she pressed, 'you urge me to pursue my own desire in defiance of His, though it is wrong to oppose the Beloved's Will.'

31. Sofyān Thawri once asked Rābe'ah whether there was anything she desired. "Though you are a man of learning," she retorted, "still you ask me questions like that! What kind of talk is this? You are aware of how inexpensive figs and dates are in Basra. Though I have desired fresh dates for twelve years, I haven't yet eaten one. I am a mere slave; what has a slave to do with desire? For if God was not in accord with my desire, this would be pure infidelity (*kofr).*".

Sofyān replied, "You've dumbfounded me. I've nothing left to say concerning your work. Speak of mine though," he requested.

"If it weren't that you love the world, Sofyān, you would be a good man," Rābe'ah answered.

"How so?" asked the scholar.

"You love reciting Traditions," Rābe'ah replied, implying that this itself was a form of status-seeking.

Deeply moved Sofyān cried, "O Lord! Be content with me!"

"Aren't you embarrassed to request someone to be content with you," Rābe'ah replied, "when you yourself are not content with Him?"

In the *Sharḥ-e ta'arrof,* this response is interpreted

by Kalābādhi as a reference to the Koranic verse, "God is content with those who are content with Him." [V:119] That is, God is content with the servent in proportion to the servent's resignation to God's will.

32. Mālek Dinār has described Rābe'ah's life-style as follows:

> I visited the saint. She possessed a pitcher with a crack in it which she employed both for ablutions and drinking; in lieu of a pillow, she used a brick. There was also an old straw mat. My heart was anguished at the sight, and I pleaded with her, 'I have wealthy friends; only indicate it and I'll see that they regard you favorably.'
>
> 'You are wrong Mālek,' she replied, 'my Provider is their Provider too, isn't He?'
>
> 'Of course,' I replied.
>
> 'Do you imagine,' she rejoined, 'that He has forgotten the poor because of their poverty, while assisting the rich because they are wealthy?'
>
> 'No,' I answered.
>
> 'Since He is cognizant of my state then,' she went on, 'what need is there to remind Him? If this is how He likes it, my wish is one with His.'

33. Ḥasan al-Basri, Mālek Dinār, and Shaqiq Balkhi once went together to confer with Rābe'ah. The subject of sincerity *(ṣedq)* was the focus of their conversation.

"Whoever does not exhibit fortitude before his Beloved's lash," Ḥasan commented initially, "is not truly sincere (*ṣādeq)* in his claim."

"There is a hint of egotism in these words,"

Rābe'ah observed.

Shaqiq ventured next, saying, "Whoever shows no thankfulness at his Master's chastisement is not truly sincere in his claim."

"Still better should be said," Rābe'ah commented.

Mālek Dinār then proferred his opinion, "Whoever does not endure his Master's scourge with delight is not sincere in his claim."

"This too can still be improved on." Rābe'ah noted.

"Then you tell us," they entreated together.

"One is not truly sincere in one's claim unless one forgets the pain of the chastisement in contemplation of one's Master. Nor should this be cause for astonishment either, just as the women of Egypt were senseless to their self-inflicted wounds when beholding Joseph. Why wonder if someone exhibits a similar character in contemplation of the Creator?" declared Rābe'ah.

34. One of the religious scholars[1] of Basra came to visit Rābe'ah. After sitting beside her couch of convalescence, he started to revile the world.

"You love the world greatly," observed Rābe'ah, "otherwise you would not remember it so frequently. Your constant reference to the world merely testifies to the truth of the proverb, 'Whoever loves a thing remembers it frequently.' "

[1]Instead of "one of the religious scholars," Ebn Jawzi in the *Ṣefat aṣ-ṣafwat* states that Riyāḥ al-Qaysi, Sālaḥ Ebn 'Abd al-Jalil, and Kolāb went to visit Rābe'ah and began reviling the world.

35. Ḥasan al-Basri recounts, "I was once in Rābe'ah's company near the time of evening prayer. She was preparing a meat dish for our dinner and had just laid the food in the pot."

"This conversation is more delightful than cooking," she commented, putting the pot aside, away from the fire, until the end of the ritual prayer. After the prayer was completed, she set a few crusts of bread before us with a pitcher of water to break our fast. She then approached the kettle to serve the meat; it was boiling, by the Power of God. She proceeded to serve the meat, and we enjoyed the meal with a relish such as I had never before experienced. With respect to this, Rābe'ah commented, "That is how those who pray prepare their food."

36. Some people asked Rābe'ah, "Where do you come from?"

"From the other world," she responded.

"Where are you going?" they pressed.

"To the other world," she replied.

"In this world, what are you doing?" they questioned.

"I mock it," she said.

"How so?" they inquired.

"This world's bread I consume," she explained, "while occupied with the affairs of the hereafter."

"So beautifully expressed!" all exclaimed. "You should be a chamberlain."

"I am already," Rābe'ah retorted, "for I do not let what is inside me go out, nor do I allow what is outside me to come in. If someone enters, he goes and has nothing to do with me. I am a chamberlain of the heart, not a lump of clay."

37. Rābe'ah was asked, "Do you love God?"
"Yes," she affirmed.
"Are you an enemy of Satan?" they inquired further.
Rābe'ah confessed. "My love of the all-Merciful leaves me no room for hostility towards Satan."

38. "Once I beheld the Prophet in a dream," Rābe'ah has related. "He asked if I loved him. 'Who doesn't love you,' I told him, 'but my heart is so totally transported with God's love that no place for love or hate of another remains'. "

The Arab historian, Zobaydi[1] in the *Etteḥāf al-sādat al-mottaqin* , renders the above anecdote in the following fashion:

> Rābe'ah was asked, 'How much do you cherish the Prophet of God?'
> 'Excessively...I love him indeed,' Rābe'ah avowed, 'but the Love of the Creator inhibits me from love of His creatures.'

39. Rābe'ah was questioned about Love (*maḥabbatt).* "Love," she pronounced, "has emanated from pre-eternity (*azal),* passed unto post-eternity (*abad)* and perceived no one among the eighteen worlds competent to imbibe even a draught of its sherbet.

---

[1]His full name was Moḥammad Ebn 'Abd al-Razzāq, surnamed Abu Fayaḍh Ḥosseini Yemāni Hanafi. He was born in 1145 and died in 1205. His family were natives of Wasit. His birthplace was in Begram, India. He was educated and raised in Zobaid, in Yemen. (Dekhoda Dictionary)

When at last Love reached the Truth, only this maxim remained: 'He Loves them and they Love Him.' "[1]

40. It is related that Rābe'ah was engaged in continual wailing and lamentation. "For what are you weeping?" she was questioned.

"My deepest fear," she confessed, "is separation, for I have become accustomed to Him. Is it not possible that at the time of death a voice will come saying, 'You are not worthy of Me?' "

41. Rābe'ah once was asked, "When does a slave acquire contentment?" She replied, "When he or she is as grateful for adversity as for bounty."

42. Again, she was asked, "Is the repentance of a sinner acceptable or not?" "How may anyone repent," she responded, "unless the Lord bestows penitence upon him, and then in consequence accepts his repentance. Till penitence be granted by Him, no one may repent."

The moral dilemma noted by Rābe'ah above has been described by the Persian poet Sa'di (d. 1291) in his *Bustan,* as follows:

> *How lovely that wretched dervish moaned each*
> *morning—his evening penitence*
> *broken by another sin.*
> *"All our oaths are empty, our vows inconstant:*
> *the repentance of His giving*
> *alone remains steadfast.*

[1]The Koranic passage (V:54) is as follows: "Whoso of you becometh a renegade from his religion, Allah will bring a people whom He loves and who love Him in return." (ed.)

43. "O children of Adam!" Rābe'ah declared, "Your eyes provide no passage to perceive the Truth, nor is there any access to Him by speech of the tongue. The faculty of hearing is but a highway to distress for the speaker, while your hands and feet only steer you only into bewilderment. The true work is in the heart. Try to acquire an awakened heart, for when the heart is awakened, it will have no need of a friend.

That is to say, an awakened heart is one which is lost in God. What need does one who is effaced and lost in God have of a friend; for this is the station of Annihilation in God" (*fanā fi'l-llāh*).

44. "Asking forforgiveness out loud," stated Rābe'ah, "is the work of hypocrites. Though we repent, we need still another repentance to repent of repenting."

45. Rābe'ah once observed, "If the virtue of patience were a man, he would be of a generous disposition."

46. Rābe'ah was once asked, "Do you actually see Him whom you worship?"

"I would not worship Him," she replied, "unless I saw Him."[1]

47. Another of Rābe'ah's statements was, "The fruit of gnosis is to turn one's face towards God, the All-Mighty."

[1] *Cf.*, 'Ali's famous adage, "I do not adore a God I cannot see."

48. "The gnostic," Rābe'ah once pronounced, "is someone who seeks a heart from God. Once this is granted to him, however, he immediately renders it back to God, such that it remains secure in His tenure and is shrouded from human access in Divinity's mystery (*serr).*"

49. Describing an overnight visit with Rābe'ah, Sofyān Thawri has written, "I saw her enter her oratory (*meḥrāb)* and occupy herself in prayers until daybreak. In the opposite corner of the house I also performed prayer till dawn. With the sunrise, she suggested we dedicate the rest of the day to fasting to express our gratitude for the grace through which we maintained the night vigil."

50. Ṣāleḥ Merri often used to say, "The door will be opened to whomever knocks."

Overhearing him once, Rābe'ah remarked, "How long will you say: 'The door will be opened...' as if it were ever closed!"

Ṣāleḥ was forced to confess, "I am a man, but an ignorant fool, while she is a weak woman but full of wisdom."

51. After her death, Rābe'ah appeared in a certain person's dream. "Tell us of Monkar and Nakir, the two angels of death," the person begged.

"Those two noble beings appeared to me," she related, and asked, 'Who is your Lord?' " I said, "Return and tell God... among so many thousands of people, You did not forget an old woman, and so, since I could never forget You who are all I have in the whole world, how then could You send someone to ask, 'Who is your Lord?' "*(Tadhkerat al-auliyā)*

52. During Rābe'ah's last hours, the masters of her age gathered around her deathbed. She commanded, "Rise and make way for the prophets of God." Rising, they left the room and shut the door. A voice was then heard declaring:

> *O soul at peace, return unto thy Lord, well-pleassed, well-pleasing!*
> *Enter thou among My servants!*
> *Enter thou My Paradise!*[1] [LXXXIX:27-29]

Nothing else was heard. The shaikhs then entered and found her dead. *(Ibid.)*

53. Moḥammad Ebn Aslam al-Ṭusi and Na'mā Ṭarsusi (God's grace be upon them), who were known to have provided water for thirty thousand people in the desert, once visited Rābe'ah's grave. They asked, "O you who boasted you would never lower your brow before anyone in the two worlds, how are you now?" They were answered by a voice saying, 'How sweet indeed was what I saw!' "

---

[1]Arberry's translation, Koran. LXXXIX:27-29. These lines are addressed to the soul that has lived a life of goodness (ed.).

54. "Once I visited Rābe'ah," relates Ḥasan al-Basri, "but this lady of her day was engaged in prayers. I knelt next to her prayer-mat for a long time observing her. Protruding from her right eye was a broken thorn and a drop of blood was trickling off her cheek onto her prayer-mat. After she finished prayers I exclaimed, "What have you come to? A thorn in your eye, your prayer-mat blood-stained..." Rābe'ah rejoined, 'O Ḥasan, I vow by God's glory, which has endowed this least of creatures with Islam's elevation, that I was utterly unconscious of this state. My heart was so taken from me, that if all the torments throughout all the stories of hell were fitted upon a needle and my right eye lined with them, were my left eye to twitch even once with that pain, I would pluck it out from its base.' " (*Tafsir-e Anṣari*, Vol. 1, p. 514)

55. The angel of death once approached Rābe'ah. She asked who he was.

"I am the destroyer of delights," he replied, "the orphaner of children, the widower of wives."

Rābe'ah then asked, "Why do you only speak of your bad qualities? Why don't you say rather, 'I am the one who unites friend with Friend.' " (*Tafsir Anṣari* , Vol. I, p. 44)

56. Rābe'ah once said: "Infidelity *(kofr)* has the flavor of separation *(farāq),* while faith *(imān)* has the delight of union *(wesāl).* This flavor and this delight will be revealed tomorrow, on the Judgment Day. The punishment of one group gathered on that plain is said to be a separation without union, while this farther company is said to possess a union without end. Those

flaming in separation's bereavement cry out:

Separation from Him turns
A single second into a thousand days;
And from his suffering and grief,
One night becomes a thousand years.

While those illumined by Divine Union affirm:

Come the day of consummation
When from before your Union's inner courtyard
The curtain was cast aside
Then distance from the Friend pounded its hand
Upon the drum of death and separation.
(*Tafsir-e Anṣāri*, Vol. II, p. 538)

57. A company of gnostics, enlightened in heart, once saw Rābe'ah running. In one hand she carried a burning brand, and in the other a pail of water. They asked, "O Lady of the after-life, where are you going, what are you doing?"

Rābe'ah replied, "I am going to set Heaven afire and put out Hell's flames. In this way the voyagers to God can surmount both these veils and clearly see the real goal. Then, devoid of ulterior motives, all slaves may truly serve God. Right now you cannot find anyone who truly worships God for his own sake, without hope for Paradise and fear of hell." (Aflāki, *Manāqeb al-'ārefin*)

58. While visiting Rābe'ah one day, Sofyān Thawri lifted his hands in supplication and prayed, "Lord, grant me well-being *(salāmat)*." Rābe'ah suddenly burst out weeping.

"Why are you crying?" Sofyān inquired.

"It is you who have made me weep," retorted Rābe'ah.

"How so?" he asked.

"Because you are unaware," replied Rābe'ah, "that well-being within the world stems from giving it up, while you are defiled by it." (Jāmi, *Nafaḥāt al-ons;* Ebn Jawzi, *Ṣefat aṣ-ṣafwat)*

59. Sofyān Thawri once inquired of Rābe'ah, "What is the best means by which a slave may aspire to be near to God?" In answer, Rābe'ah said, "That he knows the slave loves none other than Him, whether in this world or hereafter." (Jāmi, *Nafaḥāt al-ons)*

60. Rābe'ah also stated, "I grieve not because I am sorrowful; I am aggrieved at my own lack of sorrow." (Jāmi, *Nafaḥāt al-ons)*

61. It is related that Rābe'ah once dug a grave for herself at home. It was her practice to stand by the grave's edge, morning and evening, saying, "Tomorrow here you shall be." She would then engage herself in devotions. For forty years she maintained this routine until her death. (Ebn Karbalā'i, *Rawḍhāt al-jenān,* Vol. I, p. 192)

62. Sajaf Ebn Manẓur relates, "I came into Rābe'ah's presence and found her prostrated in prayer. When she sensed my presence she raised her head, and I noticed that a pool of tears had formed where her head had previously rested. After I had saluted her, she turned her face toward me and said, "My son, what is it

that you wish?" I replied, "Only to extend my greetings to you." Upon hearing this, she wept and said, "May God conceal that which is within you." She then prayed at some length on my behalf, and having done so, returned to her obligatory prayer." (Ebn Jawzi, *Ṣefat aṣ-ṣafwat*)

63. One of Rābe'ah's best known statements was, "I ask God for forgiveness for my lack of sincerity in asking for forgiveness."[1] (Ebn Jawzi, *Ṣefat aṣ-ṣafwat)* According to Abu Moḥammad Rowaim, "Rābe'ah understood the true meaning of *tawḥid* when she declared, 'I beg God's pardon for my lack of sincerity in asking God to forgive me,' her implication being that to be truly sincere in one's spiritual transactions, one must beg for God's pardon with an exterior (vocal) prayer until the *reality* of forgiveness is attained. For when there is not sincerity in one's transaction, the outer petition for forgiveness actually becomes sinful. Thus there is no real repentance, because in truth the transaction is conducted out of habit." (*Kholāsa-ye Sharḥ-e Ta'arrof)*

64. Once, Rābe'ah was passing by a company of people when they suddenly recognized her. A man among them pleaded, "Pray for me." Rābe'ah leaned up against a wall and replied, "May God Himself forgive you; who am I (to intercede)? Obey your God and invoke Him, for it is He who gives answer to all those who are afflicted." (Ebn Jawzi, *Ṣefat aṣ-ṣafwat)*

---

[1]The reference is to a supplication invoked several times a day by oridnary Muslims, begging forgiveness (ed.).

65. Once in Rābe'ah's company, Sofyān Thawri exclaimed, "O how great is my sorrow!" Rābe'ah reprimanded him saying "Don't lie. Say rather, 'how little is my sorrow;' for were you truly sorrowful, you could not have passed life with such satisfaction." (Ebn Jawzi, *Ṣefat aṣ-ṣafwat)*

The above narrative is also cited by Qoshairi *(Op. cit.)* with a slightly different conclusion.; "Were you truly sorrowful," Qoshairi quotes Rābeah as saying, "you could never have drawn a breath."

66. It is said that Rābe'ah once admonished Sofyān Thawri, saying, "Indeed your days are numbered, for when one day passes, a significant portion of your life has passed away. And when that portion has fled, soon it will come to pass that your whole life has disappeared. As you know this, strive always towards the performance of good deeds." (Ebn Jawzi, *Ṣefat aṣ-ṣafwat)*

67. Mesma' Ebn 'Aṣam and Rabāḥ al-Qaysi were in Rābe'ah's company one day when someone appeared with an offering of forty dinars. "Take this money," the man urged, "and spend it according to your needs." Rābe'ah began to weep and lifting her head heavenwards exclaimed, "You well know that it causes me shame to request the world from God, its Sovereign: how then can I accept it from one who is not its Master?" (Ebn Jawzi, *Ṣefat aṣ-ṣafwat)*

68. 'Abda bent Abi Showāl, a pious lady in Rābe'ah's service, has narrated the following account:

> Rābe'ah used to pray all night, only then permitting herself to doze lightly before dawn until the shadow of daybreak tinted the horizon. Then she would rise and I would hear her say , possessed by a deep awe, 'O base soul, how long shall you go on with sleeping and waking? The time is nigh when you will fall into such a slumber that only the trumpet call of the Resurrection will summon you awake.' This arduous routine was her way of life until she died.

At the time of her death, Rābe'ah summoned 'Abda into her presence and gave the injunction that none be informed of her death. She requested that she be shrouded only in an old gown (*jobbah*)[1] for burial. Her servant faithfully complied with her request and clothed her corpse only in that gown, covered by the woolen cloak that was her normal garb.

About a year after Rābe'ah's death 'Abdah dreamt of her. Rābe'ah appeared attired in a green silken gown embroidered with gold and silver. 'Abda had never before beheld anyone more beautiful. "What happened," the girl asked Rābe'ah, "to the old gown and woolen cloak that we buried you in?" Rābe'ah answered, "I swear by God, those garments were taken away from me, and then I was garbed in that which you see now, while my former shroud was folded, sealed and borne aloft to a sublime spot so that my reward would be perfect on the Day of Resurrection."

---

[1] A kind of hair robe, usually used for sleeping and praying at night (ed.).

"Was this the reason for all your spiritual combat (*mojāheda)* during your days on earth?" asked 'Abda. Rābe'ah answered, "What is even this compared to what I have seen of God's Munificence to His friends."

"Whatever became of 'Abda, Abu Kalāb's daughter?" 'Abdah inquired.

"Ah, far, far beyond me is the station she attained," Rābe'ah responded, "Never shall I approach her." 'Abdah pressed, "But how is this, since your spiritual state was higher than hers?" Rābe'ah rejoined, "Because she did not concern herself with how she passed her days and nights."

"And of Abu Mālek Zaygam," 'Abdah continued, "whatever became of him?" Rābe'ah replied, "He makes pilgrimage to God, the Exalted, whenever he wishes." 'Abdah further inquired concerning Bashir Ebn Manṣur.

"His state is happy," answered Rābe'ah, "for God has bestowed upon him more than he ever aspired to."

'Abdah in the end requested Rābe'ah, "Provide me with some admonition so I may draw closer to God." Rābe'ah counseled her, "Devote yourself totally to the remembrance of God, for only this shall cheer you in the grave." (Ebn Jawzi, *Ṣefat aṣ-ṣafwat)*

69. It is reported that while performing the pilgrimage to Mecca Rābe'ah remarked, "Here is the House (*Ka'ba*) which is idolized upon the earth, whereas God neither enters it nor leaves it." (Abdo'r-Ra'uf Monāwi, *Tabaqāt al-auliya)*

70. "What is your definition of generosity (*sekhā)* ?" Rābe'ah asked Sofyān Thawri. He replied, "For this

world's inhabitants, generosity consists in giving away one's possessions; for those of the world beyond, generosity amounts to sacrificing one's soul." Rābe'ah objected, saying he was mistaken. "Then what," Sofyān entreated, "is your understanding of generosity?" Rābe'ah pronounced, "Generosity is to worship Him for love of Himself alone, not to attain a reward or benefit." (Monāwi, *Tabaqāt al-auliyā)*

71. Once Rābe'ah accidently struck her head against a sharp stone in a wall. Though she began to bleed profusely, she was utterly unconscious of her condition. People asked, "Don't you feel any pain?" Rābe'ah rejoined, "I was so preoccupied with fulfilling God's will during that instant, that no sensation of what you witnessed remained to me." (Monāwi, *Tabaqāt al-auliyā)*

72. Upon overhearing someone chant the Koranic verse, "Verily on that day, Heaven's inhabitants will be joyously occupied." (LV:3), Rābe'ah observed, "The poor inhabitants of Heaven! To be busy, with their spouses." Ebn 'Arabi criticizes this adage of Rābe'ah saying, "She has not understood. It is she who is poor! For what occupies the inhabitants of Heaven is only God."

Ebn 'Arabi further states, "This (saying) refers to God's hidden guile (*makr)* in relation to the gnostics (*'ārefān)*, which causes them to find faults and make objections to other saints who are pure of such accusations."

Despite this, Ebn 'Arabi elsewhere praises Rābe'ah highly, asserting that she is of the same spiritual degree as Shaikh 'Abdo'l-Qāder Gilāni, and that there exist two distinct types of wayfarers to God whose intentions are legitimate:

> One's group's aspirations center around the Prophet as awakener and teacher of the path to Truth. In spite of this knowledge, however, they overlook the practical application of this principle, creating a space between themselves and God. Viewing no creatures before their feet, they make great strides in traversing the Path, excelling others in virtue, for they have cast out from their hearts all but God and become one with the Truth.

Ebn 'Arabi adds, "The state of the first group is possessed by Shaikh 'Abdo'l-Qāder, Abu Mas'ud Ebn Shebli, and Rābe'ah al-'Adawiya, as well as their followers. The second group holds the belief that no way exists to God but through the Prophet. They never do anything unless they behold the Prophet's footsteps before them." (Monāwi, *Tabaqāt al-auliyā)*

73. A swarm of locusts once descended upon Rābe'ah's newly planted garden. She made the supplication. "O God, you have promised me my daily sustenance; bestow it as You will, upon Your friends or enemies." At that moment, the locusts all took flight. Afterwards, it was as if they had never landed. (Monāwi, *Tabaqāt al-auliyā)*

74. "Even if the entire world belonged to one man, " Rābe'ah once observed, he would not be rich."

"How so?" she was asked.

"Because," Rābe'ah affirmed, "the world passes away." (Monāwi, *Tabaqāt al-auliyā)*

75. Rābe'ah al-'Adawiya said, "All people are afraid of the reckoning of the Day of Judgement, whereas I long for it." When she was asked why she longed for it, she replied, "Will it not be at last that God will address me as 'O, My servant!' " (Moḥammad Ebn 'Othmān, *Ferdaws al-morshidiya,* p.212)

76. Moḥammad Ebn Solaimān Hāshemi, the Governor of Baghdad, whose properties produced an income of eight thousand dirhams each day, once wrote to the nobles of Basra, requesting them to find him a suitable wife. They sought out Rābe'ah as a possible candidate. In answer to his request, Rābe'ah wrote to the Amir, "Just as abstinence (*zuhd)* in this world is a source of bodily comfort, likewise attention to the world results in worry and grief. Lay aside your excess wealth, dedicate your riches here to the life hereafter. Be trustee of your own soul now; do not let men administer and divide your wealth later on. Fast from life; let death break your fast. As for me, even if God were to place at my disposal as much as you offer, or even much more, it would not be possible for me to heed ought beside Him for as much as the wink of an eye." (Monāwi, *Tabaqāt al-auliyā)*

77. "With all these acts of devotion," Rābe'ah was asked, "What are you seeking?" She responded, "I am not after any reward for my good works, but only that on the Day of Judgment the Prophet Moḥammad should say to the rest of the Prophets: 'Behold this

woman of my community; this was her work'." (Monāwi, *Tabaqāt al-auliyā)*

78. Mālek Ebn Dinār relates how he visited Rābe'ah and found her occupied in admonishing herself: "How many passions are there, O God, whose delights perish, while only an evil after-effect remains. O Lord, shall Your sole retribution also be bad? Do You hold no other punishment besides fire?" (Monāwi, *Tabaqāt al-awliā)*

79. Sofyān Thawri once addressed Rābe'ah, saying, "Every contract has certain binding conditions, and behind every faith exists a substantial reality. What is the reality of your faith?" Rābe'ah replied, "Neither fear of Hellfire nor hope of a Heavenly reward excites my love and worship of God. If either were so, I would only be a bad employee working from fear of punishment or hope of benefit. My longing and love, rather, is the sole basis of my devotion to Him." (Zobaydi, *Itteḥāf al-sādat as-mottaqin)*

80. Rābe'ah has said, "The lover of God will cry and weep until he finds rest in the Beloved's embrace." (Shehāb al-Din 'Omar Sohrawardi, *Awārifuo'l-ma'āref,* p. 507)

81. Once Rābe'aḥ beheld Rabāḥ al-Qaysi carrying a relative's child. She inquired if he liked the child. "Yes," he affirmed. Rābe'ah commented, "Never would I have imagined that there was a place in your heart available for love of other than God." Hearing this, Rabaḥ al-Qaysi swooned. He remarked upon

recovery, "God the Almighty instills the love of infants in the hearts of His servants." (Abu No'aim Eşfahāni, *Ḥelyat al-āuliyā')*

82. "Are the nights and days long for you?" Rabāḥ al-Qaysi was asked by Rābe'ah.

"For what reason would they be?" he demanded.

"Out of your yearning to behold God."

Upon hearing this, Rabāḥ al-Qaysi remained silent.

"For me the answer is 'yes' " Rābe'ah exclaimed. *(Ḥelyat al-āwliyā)*

83. According to Abu Ali Faqih, Rābe'ah was once asked, "How did you attain that which you attained?"

"Through this," replied the saint, "that I often prayed, 'I take refuge in You, O God, from all that distracts me from You, and from every obstacle that impedes me from reaching You.' "(Monawwar, *Asrār at-tauḥid)*

84. Ḥammād has related how Salām Ebn Abu Moṭi' and he once visited Rābe'ah. Salām spoke of the world. Rābe'ah commented, "One should only mention things that exist, not things that are nothing." (Shams ad-Din Dhahabi, *Sair a'lām an-nobalā')*

85. According to 'Abdo'l-Wāḥed Zayd, Rābe'ah often frequented the congregation of Samiṭ 'Ajlān with him. The fame of her devotions caused 'Abdo'l-Wāḥed to desire her in marriage. "I expessed my wish to Samiṭ 'Ajlān, relates 'Abdo'l-Wāḥed, who said he would try to communicate my proposal to Rābe'ah. I took leave

of Samiṭ and sought her out. When I found her, she was chewing on a crust of dry bread. 'Rābe'ah,' I entreated her, 'is it bread crusts that you eat?' Facing me, she demanded, 'Which passion, O man, have you perceived in me that has caused you to yearn after me?' This shocked me, for I was certain no news of my proposal had been given to her. She then raised her face to the heavens and implored, 'O Lord, send us a pitcher of white honey for our repast.' At once, a pitcher, whose equal I had never seen, appeared out of nowhere. 'O 'Abdo'l-Wāḥed, ' Rābe'ah cried, 'if you wish for that honey which has never come forth from any bee, nor has ever been handled by any creature, then stretch out your hand and feast yourself.' I was too awe-struck to reach out my hand, however much I tried. Rābe'ah then commanded that we rise. We both did so and departed." (*Montakheb rawnaq al-majāles)*

86. People reproached Rābe'ah's master, saying, "How is it that you continue to maintain such a slave in a mere ruin?" In response to their objections, her master sought out Rābe'ah and informed her that he had arranged for a house to be put at her disposal in order that she be better able to practice her devotions. Rābe'ah assented and moved in. After a few days had passed, however, she began to feel oppressed and heavy at heart at the elaborate furnishings and at having to close the door whenever she left the house. "If God were to address me," Rābe'ah speculated, "He would say, 'O My devotee, without any house, your heart was engaged in Our remembrance, while now as owner of a house and chattels, you have severed your heart from Us.' How, then, would I respond?" After

thinking this, she returned the keys to her master and went back to her former home among the ruins. (*Montakheb rawnaq al-majāles*)

87. Sickness once motivated Rābe'ah to abandon her nightly recitation of the Koran. After regaining her health, she neglected to resume these recitations. Shortly afterwards, she had a dream:

> I found myself in a green park, lovely beyond all understanding. In the park was a maiden. I remarked to her, 'How pleasant is this place!' She asked me, 'Would you enjoy seeing someplace lovelier than this?' I answered, 'Yes,' and she took my hand and guided me to a palace, the like of which no eye had ever beheld. The maiden then knocked on a door. Upon its opening, a light was cast forth and both of us entered. Only God Almighty knows the significance of such maidens as I saw therein. In the hand of each was a light-filled serving tray. My companion asked the maidens where they were going. 'We seek someone,' they replied, 'who was drowned in the sea, as a martyr. She was ever sleepless at night; we are going to perfume her.'
>
> 'Then anoint this woman also,' my companion enjoined.
>
> 'Before,' they replied, 'a portion of this sweet fragrance and grace adhered to her, but she drew away.' The maiden then disengaged her hand from mine and said:

Your prayers are a light to you,
Your devotion, strength.
Your sleep is your prayer's bitter enemy
Your life is an opportunity;
If you neglect it and ignore it,
You will but pass into dust.

The maiden then disappeared.

According to 'Omar Ebn 'Othmān, having seen this dream, Rābe'ah never slept again at night. (*Montakheb rawnaq al-majāles*)

88. Rābe'ah's reputation for sanctity had spread far and wide among people when one night in an assembly three or four people began to ridicule and deride her. "Such a woman has set herself up," they remarked, "to make an outcry and attract public attention to herself. Let us go tomorrow and subject her to examination."

In the early morning, dressed in fancy travelling attire, they went to Rābe'ah's house and asked for admittance. A servant greeted the party and informed them that Rābe'ah was occupied in her morning devotions; she asked them to be patient for an hour. All professed to have just come from Mt. Lebanon as pilgrims, seeking a meeting with Rābe'ah. The servant heard their tale and responded, "O devotees, I have wept so much in order to sympathize with Rābe'ah that my eyes are ill. Won't you all breathe upon my eyes that by the grace of your breath, I may regain my original sight." They all feigned giving her their blessing by breathing upon her eyes. By the will of the Almighty, however, at once the eyesore of Rābe'ah's servant was healed and her vision restored.

Strengthened by what she had seen, the servant entered the house and said, "Guests have arrived from Mt. Lebanon; the blessing of their breaths has restored my ailing sight." The visitors, however, had recognized God's artifice in this and turned in reproach towards one another, exclaiming, "We are liars coming here; it is God alone, the Exalted, who could perform such a subtle work. Had we come here in sincerity, though, imagine what our state would be!" At that moment, they all repented, donated their wealth to the poor and entered among the company of the saints. (*Montakheb rawnaq al-majāles)*

89. "On hearing that Rābe'ah was ill," related Abu Bakr Mofasser, "I accompanied a party of friends going to visit her. When we arrived, I inquired after her health. 'Death,' she told us, 'is a bridge between friends. The time now nears that I cross that bridge, and friend meets Friend.' " (*Montakheb rawnaq al-majāles)*

90. Rābe'ah possessed a frock (*moraqqa')* which she wore while praying. Much has been related about the charismatic grace of that frock. As an example, it is said that Hajjāj (an Umayyad general famous for his cruelty) had appointed a corrupt man as governor of Baghdad. People advised Rābe'ah of his injustice and entreated her to pray that they be immune from his oppression.

"He will perish," Rābe'ah remarked, "if I engage in the least supplication. Instead I shall admonish him. Perhaps thus he will repent and return to obedience." Rābe'ah then handed her frock to one of her pupils and said, "Give this to the Amir and inform him that Rābe'ah sends her greetings. Relay to him that this frock is much obliged to me for the service I have performed for God in it. When I depart from this world, however, I must leave this frock behind since I am very weak and own no horses. I have been told that you possess many horses. Put this frock on one of your horses and hand it back to me on the far side of the bridge across Hell."

Having received this message from Rābe'ah's pupil, the governor clasped the frock and rubbed his face in it, exclaiming, "O Rābe'ah you have awakened me with a whip." Then he made penance, returned to his subjects their unlawfully seized property and joined the company of the pious. (*Montakheb rawnaq al-majāles)*

91. Once a thief entered Rābe'ah's cottage, but could find only a water-pot. As he made to leave, Rābe'ah chided him saying, "If you are really a fearless thief, don't go away without pilfering something." The thief replied that he could find nothing to steal.

"Here then, take this water pot," Rābe'ah enjoined him, "perform your ritual ablutions (*wozu')*, and go into that side room and recite two *rak'ats* of prayer. If you act as such, you will never leave empty-handed."

The thief followed Rābe'ah's counsel. As he stood to pray, Rābe'ah raised her head to heaven and implored, "My Sire and Lord, this thief has entered my home, but found nothing to take from me. I showed him the door of your mansion; do not bar him from your goodness and bounty."

Upon termination of the two *rak'at* of prayer, the

thief discovered his devotion to have caused him great delight, and so continued praying until morning. Rābe'ah entered his chamber at sunrise; the thief was still bowed in prostration, his forehead touching the earth. The thief seemed to be engaged in desperately deriding his *nafs*, reciting:

If my Creator asks me,
Aren't you ashamed yet of your disobedience
towards Me?
In wickedness you run toward Me
While from men I hide your sins.
When He admonishes and sends me away,
What shall I say then to Him?

"How did you spend the night, my friend?" inquired Rābe'ah.

"Oh quite well," the thief replied, his face beaming in astonishment. "I saw myself abased before God, in misery and wretchedness. He accepted my repentance, restored me from disintegration, redeemed me from contrition and forgave my sins, such that I attained to what I sought."

In supplication, Rābe'ah raised her hands toward heaven and prayed, "O my Master, my Lord, this person stood by Your door for the span of an hour and was admitted, and I, from the instant I encountered You have never sensed myself absent from Your presence. Shall I behold myself also some day among the company of those who were admitted?" Within her deepest conscience a voice replied, "For your sake, Rābe'ah, We admitted him, and have caused him to draw near to Us." (Arabic MS. 1242, p. 183, Vatican Library)

92. Once Rābe'ah was asked for some insight concerning Love *(maḥabbat).* "No separation exists," she responded, "between the Beloved and the lover." ('Ezzo'd-Din Ebn 'Abdo's-Salām Ebn Ghānem al-Moqaddasi, *Sharḥ ḥāl al-auliyā,* Arabic MS. 1641 in the Paris Public Library)

93. "O Rābe'ah," people said, "you who surpass everyone in the sphere of Divine Love *(maḥabbat).* Why did they name you 'the Fourth' (*ar-rābe'ah)?* Since the Object is One, whence all this multiplicity and this associating others with God?"

Rābe'ah retorted, "In faring the Path of spiritual companionship *(ṭariq-e soḥbat)*, concordance and compatibility (*mowāfeqat)* is required."(*Sharḥ ḥāl al-auliyā)*

94. Rābe'ah was once asked, "Did you ever perform any work that, in your opinion, caused God to favor and accept you?"

She replied, "Whatever I did, I fear, may be counted against me." (Jaḥeẓ, *Al-bayān wa't-tabyin)*

95. Rābe'ah declared, "Conceal your good qualities as much as you conceal your bad qualities." (Ebn Khallekān, *Wafiyyāt al-a'yān)*

96. People questioned Rābe'ah, "Through what particular thing did you accrue the most benefit?" She replied, "All I did I count as nothing." (Shaikh Bahā'i, *Kashkul)*

97. Once a lady professed to Rābe'ah, "For God's sake,

I love you." Rābe'ah replied, "Obey Him, then, for Whose sake you love me." (Ebn Khallekan, *Wafiyyāt al-a'yān)*

98. It was Rābe'ah's habit to continually pray, "O Creator, I forgive everyone who has oppressed me for Your sake. Request whoever I have oppressed to forgive me." (Ebn Khallekan, *Wafiyyāt al-a'yān)*

99. Once a person prayed for Rābe'ah; the saint subsequently appeared in the person's dream. "Your gifts were borne up to me on trays of light," Rābe'ah related, "which were covered in a garb of light." (Ebn Khallekan, *Wafiyyāt al-a'yān)*

100. Rābe'ah enjoined her father, saying, "It isn't permissible for you to obtain my food in an unlawful manner." Her father objected, "What if I find nothing but food of unlawful nature?" Rābe'ah responded, "Far better is it to exhibit patience before hunger in this world than to tolerate the fire of the hereafter." (Ebn Khallekan, *Wafiyyāt al-ā'yān)*

101. Once Sofyān Ṯhawri paid a visit to Rābe'ah and found her distressed.

"O mother," exclaimed Sofyān, "I see these times have caused you distress. If you go to the house of such-and-such a neighbor he will help you."

Rābe'ah objected, "What have you seen, Sofyān, that causes you to call my condition bad? Is not the fact that I am a Muslim an honor without disgrace, a wealth devoid of poverty and a friendship free of fear? Truly by God, I swear it causes me shame to desire the world from the One who owns it. How then should I desire it from one who doesn't even own it." Sofyān arose and exclaimed, "Such words as these I have never heard." (Ebn Khallekan, *Wafiyyāt al-a'yān)*

102. One day Rābe'ah encountered Shaybān Rā'i and informed him that she was planning to go on a pilgrimage. Shaybān took some gold from his pocket and offered it to Rābe'ah for her journey. Rābe'ah, in response, raised her hand in the air; it soon was filled with gold.

"You take gold from your pocket," she told Shaybān, "while I gather it from the World of the Invisible (*ghayb)*".

Thus did Shaybān and Rābe'ah set out on pilgrimage with trust in God (*tawakkol)* as their only fare. (Shaikh Yusof ebn Esmā'il Nabahāni, *Jāme' karāmāt al-auliyā)*

103. Once someone mentioned a holy man of high spiritual rank in Rābe'ah's presence. All he ate, they related, was the discarded leftovers from a local prince's table. Someone commented, "What would be wrong if a man of such an exalted rank were to ask God to provide him with food in another manner?" Rābe'ah told the speaker to be quiet. "Do you not know, you senseless man," she said, "That the friends of God prefer that He alone arrange their provision, rather than wishing their sustenance to be improved outwardly for them." (Abu'ṭ-Ṭāleb Makki, *Qut al-qolub,* Vol. 2, p. 80)

104. Once a week, Ḥasan al-Basri held an assembly where he gave a sermon. When he mounted the pulpit, he would always look for Rābe'ah and, if he did not see her, would refuse to preach. The people pleaded with him, saying, "So many dignified and important people, dignitaries and nobles, have congregated here. What does it matter if one old woman in a veil doesn't come?" Ḥasan replied, "That wine which we have made for the capacity of elephants cannot be poured into the breasts of ants."

Whenever the assembly of people became warm and enthused from his words, he would turn towards Rābe'ah and say, "Ah, though concealed beneath a veil, all this passion is from but an ember in your heart." ('Aṭṭār, *Tazkerat al-āuliyā'*)

An Ecstatic Saying of Rābe'ah

Were the rapture of Divine Love which I have realized ever to be bestowed upon humankind, no one would remain unaffected by this love. (Wali'od-Din 'Abdo'r-Raḥman Ebn Khaldun, *Shafā' al-sā'il le-tahzib al-masā'il.* MS. 24299 in the library of Egypt, cited by 'Abdo'r-Raḥman Badawi, *Shahid-e 'eshq-e elahi,* p. 423)

Poems of Rābe'ah

Historically, it is not clear whether Rābe'ah actually composed the poetry attributed to her, or merely learned the poems of various poets and later recited them on appropriate occasions. The latter conjecture is more probable. Below are three of the poems in question:

I.

Within my heart I established You
As a Friend with whom I could converse;
My body I offered to one
Who wished to be next to me.
I view this body as suitable
For sitting next to, but my heart's lover
Alone befriends my heart.

II.

I have loved Thee with two loves,
a selfish love and a love that is
worthy of thee.
As for the love that is selfish, I occupy myself
Therein with remembrance of Thee to the
exclusion of all others,
As for that which is worthy of Thee,
Therein Thou raisest the veil that I may see
Thee.
Yet there is no praise to me in this or that
But the praise is to Thee, whether in that or this.

III.

How strange that you pretend to love God,
but still sin against Him.
If you love God, do His will!
For to love someone
Is to comply utterly with his will.[1]

[1] I. Abu'ṭ-Ṭāleb Makki, *Qut al-qolub;*; Zobaybi, *Itteḥāf as-sādat al-mottaqin; Meṣbāḥ al-hedāyat*, p. 423. II. The translation is buyM. Smioth, *op. cit.* pp. 102-03. It is cited by the first two sources in I. III. *Meṣbāḥ al-hedāyat*, p. 409.

The Supplications of Rābe'ah

1. "If tomorrow upon the Day of Judgment, O God, You send me to hell, I will reveal a secret such that hell will flee a thousand years from me. To Your enemies, O Lord, assign what You will of this world; assign to Your friends what You will of the hereafter—but for me, You Yourself are enough. O God! If I adore You from fear of hell, burn me in hell. If I adore You in hope of paradise, cast me out of paradise. Yet if I adore You for You alone, do not withhold your Eternal Beauty from me."

"If tomorrow You cast me into hell, in an uproar I will cry, 'Only you I have loved! Do you act such with friends?' " Here a voice responded, "Do not hold bad suspicions of Me. Think well of Me, for I have admitted you into the company of My friends, so that you may commune with Me."

She also said: "My only work, my only wish in this world, is to remember You, and in the hereafter to behold Your face. This is all there is for me; now do as You will. Either grant my heart Your presence, or accept my prayers empty of heart." ('Aṭṭār, *Tadhkerat al-auliyyā*)

The sentiments of this prayer by Rābe'ah have also been expressed in verse by 'Aṭṭār in the *Conference of the Birds:*

Omniscient Master of mysteries, invoked
Rābe'ah,
Let evil run rife, allow your enemies
To do the world's work. Unto friends
Grant everlasting life beyond.
— As for me, I'm always beyond both.

In this life or the life hereafter
If I be destitute or deprived,
If but one moment alone You befriend me--
my distress is less.
Your bounty overwhelms me,
Grand is such destitution!

Were I once to seek other than You
Or be attentive to either realm,
I'd be a faithless infidel.
To one who for His sake lives,
Everything else lives for him.
Beneath his bridge surge the seven seas.

All that is, that was or will be
Can be simulated except the Almighty
For all one seeks in life, a likeness does exist
Only He is ever unequalled to everything else.

2. At sunset Rābe'ah was accustomed to climb onto her rooftop and converse with God, saying, "My God all has quieted, and every outer motion has reached tranquillity. Every lover has secreted himself with his sweetheart. Now with You I am at last secluded. O Beloved, let my solitude with You tonight serve to save me from Hellfire hereafter." (Ebn Khallekān, *Wafiyyāt al-a'yān*)

3. It is said that after Rābe'ah had performed her evening prayers, she would climb onto the roof of her cottage in her nightgown and bonnet and beseech God, "O my Lord, the stars have all set; all eyes are fast asleep. Behind their barred gates, princes slumber. Lovers with sweethearts revel in intimate privacy. Yet, before Your face, I stand alone."

Then she would pray until dawn, and as daybreak neared, she would cry out, "O my God, another night retreats, another day shines. How I wish I knew whether You have found my passing of the night acceptable, so I may be contented, or whether You have found it inappropriate, so I may grieve. But I swear, by Your Glory, from the initial day You revived and befriended me, sleeplessness has been my constant disposition. Even if You were to drive me away from Your portal, I swear, upon Your Grandeur, I'd not be estranged because of Your love which dwells in my heart."

Then she would sing:

O my joy, my longing,
O my sanctuary, my companion,
O provision of my way
O my ultimate aim!
You are my spirit;
You are my hope;
You are my friend,
My yearning, my welfare.
Without You, O my life and love,
Never across these endless countries
Would I have wandered.
How much grace, how many gifts,
Favors and bounty have You shown me .
Your love I seek; in it I am blessed,
O radiant eye of my yearning heart!
You are my heart's captain!
As long as I live, never from You
Shall I be free. Be satisfied with me,
O my heart's desire, and I am fortunate, blessed.

(Shaikh Sho'aib al-Horaifish, *Al-rawaḍh al-fā'iq)*

1

An eighteenth century Mughal miniature. A female Sufi visiting a female hermit. B.M. 1920-9-17-090.

RABE'AH OF SYRIA

Of the esteemed women Sufi saints who attained to a high station upon the Path, Rābe'ah the Syrian is one of the most renowned. She was the daughter of Esmā'il of Syria and the wife of Aḥmad Ebn Abi al-Ḥawāri, also known as Abu'l Ḥasan or Maimun ('the Fortunate') who came from Damascus and died in 845. The latter was a contemporary and associate of some of the major Sufi masters of his day, including Abu Salaimān Dārāni (d.830), Sofyān 'Aiyana, Marwān Ebn Mo'āwiya al-Fazzāri, Boshr Ebn Asadi, and Abā 'Abdo'llah al-Nabāji. Al-Ḥawāri's brother, Mawla Ebn aba al-Ḥawāri, was renowned for his abstinence and detachment, and his son 'Abdo'llah, was a well-known ascetic. (Ebn Jawzi, *Ṣefat aṣ-ṣafwat)*

Rābe'ah was a pious devotee and ascetic. She possessed vast learning and undeniable charismatic powers. When Rābe'ah asked Aḥmad to marry her, the latter never supposed that she solely wished to please God by this action. Accordingly, he rejected her entreaty, declaring himself too preoccupied with his own spiritual devotions to consider women.

By way of rebuttal, Rābe'ah also professed herself to be too enwrapped in her own state to be attentive to him. "Nor do I have any lust for men," she swore. "Yet I have received a rather large inheritance from my husband which I desire to donate to you and your Muslim brothers. I only view you as a medium to accomplish this act of charity, as a means of becoming acquainted with people of noble conduct, and as a way of assisting myself to attain the Truth."

Aḥmad insisted on gaining his shaikh's permission

to marry and recounted, "My Master always forbade me to marry, citing how none of his companions married who did not subsequently fall far away from him." On hearing, however, that the name of Aḥmad's prospective bride was Rābe'ah, his master gave his full acquiescence and encouragement to the match, saying, "She is the perfect saint of God; her words are minted with sincerity." Aḥmad thus married her, and later on, three other women as well.[1]

In his *Ṣefat aṣ-ṣafwat*, Ebn Jawzi emphasizes that in contrast to Rābe'ah of Basra, the wife of Aḥmad Abi Ḥawāri was named 'Rāyi'ah' not 'Rābe'ah'. It is true that most historians have confused Rābe'ah of Basra with Rābe'ah of Syria, and thereby attributed tales and anecdotes about the one to the other, and vice versa. In any case, there is no doubt that Rābe'ah of Syria was the wife of Aḥmad Ebn Abi al-Ḥawāri. Those stories, then, that Aḥmad specifically relates of Rābe'ah, must be considered to refer to his own spouse.

Tales About Rābe'ah of Syria[2]

1. It is related on the word of Aḥmad Ebn Abi al-Ḥawāri that Rābe'ah one day made a meal and begged, "O sir, eat this food, for I have prepared it while engaged in praising God."

---

[1]Serāj ad-Din Abu Ḥafs 'Omar Ebn 'Ali Ebn Aḥmad Meṣri (723-804), *Tabaqāt al-auliyā*.

[2]The following tales derive from various classic texts in this order: Tales 1-6: Ebn Jawzi, *Ṣefat aṣ-ṣafwat;* Tales 7-10: Monāwi, *Tabaqāt al-auliyā'*, Tales: 11-15 Sha'rāni, Tales: 16-18 Sebṭ, Ebn Jawzi, *Mer'āt al-zamān*, MS. 1505, Bibliotheque Nationale, Paris.

2. Aḥmad also relates, "Once, when a basin was set before her, Rābe'ah commanded that it be removed, saying, 'Upon its side I see inscribed that the Commander of the Faithful, Hārun ar-Rashid is dead.' We investigated her statement and found that he had died that very day.' "

3. "A variety of mystical states *(aḥwāl)* overcame Rābe'ah," Aḥmad relates. "Sometimes Love *('eshq)* and intense affection *(maḥabbat)* prevailed, sometimes awesome fear *(khawf)*.

When overwhelemed by of Love, she would exclaim:

O my Love — like Him there is no one.
Other than Him, none may share my heart.
O my Friend — hidden to myself
From my eyes concealed, invisible
Yet from my heart never absent…

Possessed of a state of intimacy *(ons)*, Rābe'ah was accustomed to utter:

Within my heart I established you
As a Friend with whom I could converse;
My body I offered to one
Who wished to be next to me.
I view this body suitable
For sitting next to, but my heart's lover
Alone befriends my heart.[1]

[1]This poem was also attributed to Rābe'ah Al-'Adawiya of Basra.

Overcome with fear *(khawf)*, she confessed:

Should I weep for lack of provision
Or for the duration of the sojourn?
How shall I ever attain the Real Aim?
My provisions fall short.
Shall you punish me by fire,
O Ultimate Aim of all desire?
In this lies both my fear's origin
And the source of all my hope.

4. "My love for you," Rābe'ah continually reminded her husband, "is only sisterly; I do not love you as a spouse."

5. Aḥmad recounts how he once summoned Rābe'ah but received no response. An hour later she said to him, "My heart was so filled with the joy of God that I could not answer you."

6. According to Aḥmad, Rābe'ah once said, "I have always understood, O brother, that when a servant truly engages in active devotional obedience *(ṭa'at)* to God, He will disclose to him the blemishes in his behavior and concern Himself with him, prior to all creatures."

7. Aḥmad relates, "Once, when I was engaged in performing the prayers of the night vigil, I remarked to Rābe'ah that I never saw anyone remain so concentratedly awake the whole night long, as she." Rābe'ah replied, "God be glorified! Do not speak like this. When I am called, I arise."

Aḥmad has also recounted that on one occasion

while he was eating dinner, Rābe'ah called him to perform the night-long prayers. In response, he told her to go away and let him enjoy his evening meal in peace. Rābe'ah then replied, "But you and I do not belong among those who lose their appetites when remembering *(dhekr)* the next world."

8. Every night, Rābe'ah would purify herself and come before her husband saying, "Do you have any needs?" If he did, she would perform them. Then she would separate from him, make her ablutions and remain in worship till morning."

9. "Rābe'ah had seven thousand dirhams," Aḥmad recalls, "all of which she spent on me."

10. "I do not hold it to be religiously lawful *(ḥalāl),*" Rābe'ah informed her husband, "to deny you either myself or any other. Thus, you may go and choose for yourself another woman."

Aḥmad relates that he then betrothed three other women, while Rābe'ah continued to cook for him and urged him to share his food with his other wives.

11. Aḥmad has recounted, "Whenever I tried to get close to her during the day, Rābe'ah would beg me, for God's sake, not to break her fast. At night, whenever I tried to approach her, she entreated me to allow her to be exclusively devoted to God for the night."

12. Rābe'ah once confessed to Aḥmad, "Never once did I hear the prayer-call without recalling the sound of trumpets on the Judgment Day, nor do I ever watch the snow fall without remembering the fluttering of the

pages of the Book containing the deeds of those to be judged upon the Resurrection. Neither do I observe the flight of locusts without remembering the Judgment Day."

13. Aḥmad recounts, "I would become filled with awe and reverence whenever I gazed upon Rābe'ah's face. My heart would palpitate with dread whenever I saw her. Yet, when I was occupied with my companions discussing the effects of devotion in our circles of remembrance, I never sensed this sort of awe."

14. Aḥmad relates that he once overheard Rābe'ah complain, "I begrudge giving my *nafs* any good-tasting food, and I am grieved when I notice that my arms have grown plump."

15. "I often asked Rābe'ah whether or not she was fasting," Aḥmad states, "and her normal reply was, 'A woman such as myself never breaks her fast in the world.' "

16. "Once Rābe'ah handed me five dirhams," Aḥmad recalls, "and urged me, 'Take this money and acquire for yourself a new wife or buy a slave girl, for I must excuse myself from you.' "

17. "Once Rābe'ah prepared some food for me," Aḥmad recalls, "and said 'Here, you are a newly married man, eat this meat — you need it.' "

18. Abu Na'im relates the following account from Sari Saqaṭi (d. 867):

When I reached Syria, I went into a mosque and encountered Aḥmad Ebn Abi al-Ḥawāri. Giving him greetings of peace, I begged him to counsel me. 'I don't give very good advice,' he admitted, 'but you are welcome to go to my house where there is someone who delivers excellent lectures.' Upon leaving the mosque, I set out in search of al-Ḥawāri's house. On my way, however, I met a small monk who was following a big monk. 'Why are you following that fellow?' I asked the small monk.

'He is my physician, he gives me medication,' he responded. As I heard him speak, something inexplicable, beyond understanding, descended into my heart. I found al-Ḥawāri's house and knocked at the door. A woman answered, peering out at me from behind a curtain. I related to her the words of the small monk. She rejoined, 'I really wish I knew what medicine that monk bestowed — that of wakefulness or that of comfort.' When I asked her to explain more clearly what she meant, she explained, 'By the medicine of wakefulness, I mean abstinence from what God has forbidden. By the medicine of comfort, I mean contentment with God.' Her words, I swear to God, have never left my heart.

The Death of Rābe'ah of Syria

According to Ebn Jawzi *(Ṣefat aṣ-ṣafwat)*, Rābe'ah of Syria passed away in 235/850, and her grave is located on the Mount of Olives in Jerusalem. Sebṭ Ebn Jawzi (the grandson of Enn Jawzi, cited above) states in the *Mer'at az-zamān)*, however, that she died in 229/844.

OMM ḤAYYAN SALMIYAH

"I never beheld either man or woman with more perseverance in maintaining the night vigil and prayers than Omm Ḥayyān Salmiyah," states Abu Khaldah. "When she stood for prayers in the neighborhood mosque, she was so thin that she trembled like a date-palm in the breeze."

According to Savādah Salmiyah, "Omm Ḥayyān, both night and day, was engaged in the recitation of the Koran; she never spoke to anyone, except on concluding the evening prayer. She would then engage in whatever worldly business was at hand and accomplish her necessary tasks." (Ebn Jawzi, *(Ṣefat aṣ-ṣafwat)*

OMM AḤMAD, THE MIDWIFE

Omm Aḥmad was a woman of piety from Egypt, a good lady who practiced midwifery solely to satisfy the will of God, and refused to accept any payment in return for her services.

"One winter night," her son relates, "she ordered me to light the lantern. I replied that we were out of oil. She then ordered me to pour water into the lantern and remember God. I did so, and the wick caught fire. 'Mother,' I asked, 'is water really burning?' She replied, 'No son, rather whoever obeys God, all things obey him.' " (Shaikh Yusef Ebn Esmā'il Nabahāni, *(Jāme' karāmāt al-awliyā')*

ALUF MAWṢALI

"A man from Mosul once proposed marriage to Aluf Mawṣali," relates Abu Solaimān. "She responded to the messenger by saying, 'Tell him that if he were to be my slave and whatever he has were to become my property, I could never distract myself from God for his sake, even for an instant.' " (Ebn Jawzi, *Ṣefat aṣ-ṣafwat)*

OMM EBRAHIM

Omm Ebrāhim was once kicked by a horse. Her ankle was dislocated, and a company of sympathizers gathered around her. She declared, "If it weren't for all the afflictions of this world, we would all reach the hereafter utterly destitute."

Abu Musā tells the following tale of her:

> I once accompanied Omm Ebrāhim on the pilgrimage to Mecca. When we arrived at Menā, at the spot where pebbles are cast at Satan, we saw a large group of people occupied with worldly trade, buying and selling. Raising her head to the heavens, Omm Ebrāhim implored, 'O my Friend, these people have all turned toward the world and abandoned You.' Saying this, she screamed and swooned. All the people gathered around her while I shielded her with my cloak. I informed them that she had had an accident and was sick. I stood by her till she recovered consciousness. Then I raised her head and reproached her. 'O Omm Ebrāhim, why have you caused this disgrace?' She replied, 'O babbler,

when it is He himself who apportions praise and thanksgiving, why should we make a false display of ourselves?' (Ebn Jawzi, *Ṣefat aṣ-ṣafwat)*

AMENAH RAMLIYAH

Beshr Ebn al-Hāreth (d.841) was accustomed to visit Amenah Ramliyah often. Once when al-Hāreth contracted a sickness, Amenah went to visit him instead. Aḥmad Ebn Hanbal (d.838) also came to inquire after al-Hāreth's health. Noticing Amenah, Aḥmad Ebn Ḥnbal asked who she was.

"Amenah Ramliyah," replied Beshr, "who heard of my illness all the way in Ramliyah, has come to visit me."

Aḥmad Ebn Ḥanbal (d. 838) then asked Beshr to entreat her to pray for them. Amenah, in response to their request, exclaimed, "O Lord, Beshr and Aḥmad Ebn Ḥanbal seek from You security from hell-fire. O Most Merciful One, grant their prayer."

According to Aḥmad, "At the fall of night, a letter fell from the heavens upon which was inscribed: 'In the Name of the Compassionate and the Merciful. We have caused you to be immune from the fire of Hell, and even more than this is in Our power.' " (Sha'rāni, *Ṭabaqāt al-kobrā* Vol. I, p. 57; Ebn Jawzi, *Ṣefat aṣ-ṣafwāt)*

This noble woman was a pupil of the revered Māmā[1] and was buried in the same mausoleum. The author of the *Rawḑhāt al-janān* (II 54) Ebn Karbalā'i, writes:

> She was a woman of great quality and high spiritual states. Her teacher, Lady Māmā, was dominated by the attributes of majesty and wrath *(jalāl),* whereas Ajibayki was endowed with beauty and love *(jamāl).* Once, after a serious drought had afflicted the province of Azerbaijan, a Sufi had a vision in which Ajibayki gave him a loaf of bread. He found himself in a state of joy when he awoke, and soon thereafter the drought ceased.
>
> Upon the death of Ajibayki, the corpse-washer who had handled and washed the body of Māmā 'Eṣmat also washed her body. Ajibayki had worn a gold ring on her finger as payment to the mortician. Still affected by her previous experiences with Māmā, the woman made little haste in taking the ring. Yet as she was washing the body, she noticed that the baby finger of the corpse parted as if offering her the ring.
>
> She then knew that Ajibayki wanted her to take it. Kissing Ajibayki's hand, she removed the ring.

[1]See the entry for Māmā 'Eṣmat (ed.).

ACHI, THE SHAWL-WEARER

Ebn Karbalā'i writes, "Achi, the Shawl-wearer, that spiritual hero who wore the Sufi mantle, that self-aware gnostic, was buried in the vicinity of the sepulchre of Khwāja Najmo'd-Din Moḥammad[1], in Tabriz.

"Achi was a good woman and a devotee of noble character. A contemporary of the aforementioned Khwāja Najmo'd-Din, many miracles are attributed to her. She was never devoid of some mystic state. Her sepulchre is located in the Gajil graveyard and is one of the renowned tombs there." (*Rawḍhāt al-janān,* Vol. I, p. 441)

OMM ḤESAN

This lady was a renowned ascetic in Kufa, Iraq. It is related that Sofyān Thawri desired to be her husband and visited her often. Sofyān relates that upon visiting her house, he perceived nothing but an old reed mat.

"Were you only to write to your cousins," he beseeched her, "they would be more considerate of you."

Omm Ḥesān replied with this rebuke, "Sofyān, in my eyes and heart I considered you far nobler than I behold you now. I have never desired this world from the One who has sovereign authority over it; how then may I petition anything from someone who is utterly

[1]One of the great Sufi masters of Tabriz, who was subject to the spiritual influence of the Naqshbandi master, Moḥammad Pārsā (d. 1419) and passed away in 1478.

powerless? I swear by God that it is distasteful to me, O Sofyān, that I ever engage my time in anything other than God, the Almighty."[1]

Upon hearing this, Sofyān wept. (Jāmi, *Nafaḥāt al-ons.)*

OMM AYMAN, WIFE OF ABU 'ALI RUDBARI

'Azizah was the given name of this noble lady. Abu 'Abdo'r-Raḥmān Solami, on the word of one of his friends, relates that Abu 'Ali Rudbāri's wife, 'Azizah, said, "Since my ultimate return is to You, how should I not always aspire to be with You? As I never saw any good from other than You, how should I not love You? Since it is You who have set yearning within me, how should I not yearn for You?"

'Azizah is also quoted as saying, "There is no action which a devotee of God can perform as profitable and beneficial as the seeking of his lawful sustenance and livelihood."

AMAT AL-JALIL, DAUGHTER OF 'AMR 'ADAWIYA

Amat al-Jalil was a pious and saintly Arab lady. Abu Bakr Ebn 'Abid writes of her:

[1]In the *Ṣefat aṣ-ṣafwat*, Ebn Jawzi narrates a similar story on the word of 'Abdo'llah Ebn Mobārak (181 A.H.) The author of the biographical encyclopedia *Rayḥānat al-ādab* also cited the latter person, and seems to have derived his information from Jāmi, *Nafaḥāt al-ons.*

I once read in a book belonging to Moḥammad Ebn Ḥosain a notation in his own hand where he cited Ḥalim Ebn Ja'far who, in turn, quoted Mosamme' Ebn 'Asem as saying, "Once a group of Sufi masters found themselves at variance concerning the significance of saintship *(walāyat).* One remarked, 'When a servant attains to the rank of saintship, he may have whatever he wishes, be it spiritual or worldly.' Someone else said, 'The saint never acts in a way contrary to God's will, and does not strive to attain anything he may desire in the world; rather, his mere longing for it makes it materialize before him.' Still another person commented, 'The saint is one who, if not given his full rights upon the Day of Judgment, will make no objections.' Their discussions continued in this manner until finally all the shaikhs adjourned, resolving to pay a visit to a woman of the Bani' Adi tribe by the name of Amat al-Jalil, the daughter of 'Amr 'Adawiya, who was unique in her time in spiritual struggle *(mojāheda).*

Arriving at her residence, they knocked on her door and requested admittance. Once inside, they laid their differences before her and related all that had ensued in their previous debates. Amat then declared, 'A saint's times are such that he or she is so excessively absorbed and occupied with God that he or she can't be bothered with the world. Thus, the saint has no need.' Facing Kelāb, Amat then remarked, 'If someone ever tries to tell you that a saint of God ever pays attention to anything besides God, do not believe him.' " (Ebn Jawzi, *Ṣefat aṣ-ṣafwat)* [1]

---

[1]Sha'rāni in the *Ṭabaqāt al-kobra* (Vol. I, p. 57) also refers briefly to Amat al-Jalil.

Omm 'Ali, otherwise known as Fāṭemah, was the wife of Aḥmad Ebn Khaḏhruya (d. 854). She was the daughter of one of the nobles of Balkh. Although she was at one time quite wealthy, she spent all her riches on the poor *(foqarā)* and lived uncomplainingly with her husband, Aḥmad. She associated with Bayazid Basṭami (d. 874 or 877) and Abu Ḥafṣ Haddād (d. 878).

The latter relates that before encountering Omm 'Ali, he had always abhored listening to women. "I finally saw, however," he confessed, "that the Almighty lends gnosis and apprehension to whomever he pleases."

Bayazid Basṭāmi once declared, "One who struggles to practice the purity of Sufism should act with a magnanimous aspiration and demeanor like that of Omm 'Ali, wife of Aḥmad Khaḏhruya. Whoever would wish to see a true man disguised as a woman, let him see Fāṭemah."

Fāṭemah was a model on the Sufi way. Having performed penance, she sent a message to Aḥmad, asking him to request her hand in marriage from her father. Aḥmad refused, and again she sent another messenger.

"I imagined that you, Aḥmad," she chided him, "were more man-like than to waylay seekers on this Way. Be a leader, not a brigand."

In response, Aḥmad sent her an envoy with a marriage proposal addressed to her father. The latter considered their engagement a Godsend. Renouncing all connection with the world, Fāṭemah and Aḥmad lived together as recluses until both set out on a pilgrimage to Bayazid Basṭāmi.

Upon meeting Bayazid, Fāṭemah unabashedly removed her veil and sat conversing fearlessly before him. Aḥmad was astonished and became jealous at heart. "How can you be so impudent with Bayazid?" her husband later demanded.

Fāṭemah replied, "You are my physical nature's confidant and consort, Bayazid is my spiritual confidant. I attain my physical desire through you; through him I reach God. The fact that he doesn't need my company, but you do, demonstrates this."

Fāṭemah continued to behave presumptuously before Bayazid until, one day, observing a stain on her hand he remarked, "Why do you put henna on your hands?" Rebuking Bayazid, she said, "I was utterly free with you, Bayazid, so long as you never stared at my hand or commented upon its stain. But now that your eyes have started to observe my hands, all further communication between us is forbidden." Aḥmad and his wife then returned and settled in Nishapur.

When Yaḥyā Ebn Mo'ādh Rāzi (d. 258 / 859) was on his way to Balkh after returning from Ray to Nishapur, Aḥmad invited him to visit.

"Fāṭemah, how should we entertain Yaḥyā when he comes?" Ahmaḍ asked.

She replied, "This many cows and sheep should be slain, so many candles and so much perfume be prepared. Twenty donkeys should also be killed." Aḥmad said, "But what is the sense of killing donkeys, which are forbidden to Muslims?"

Fāṭemah then exclaimed, "When a generous person is a guest at the house of a generous person, shouldn't the dogs in the neighborhood be notified of his arrival?"

Fāṭemah has also said, "God, through an infinite variety of subtle graces and goodneses, invited people to Himself, but they did not respond to His call, so He afflicted them with diverse calamities, that by means of this torment they might return to Him, for He loves His creation."

Fāṭemah also declared, "It is far easier to overcome one's desires than to endure being abased by seeking after them."

It is related that a woman from Balkh once visited Fāṭemah and declared, "I wish to attain nearness to God through serving you." Fāṭemah responded, "Why not seek proximity to me through serving God?" (Adapted from 'Aṭṭar, *Tadhkerat al-auliyā'* ; Jāmi, *Nafaḥāt al-ons;* and Hojwiri, *Kashf al-maḥjub*)

OMM TALQ

Omm Talq was one of the devout women of Basra. She was reputed to perform four hundred *rak'at* of prayer each day and night, and was renowned for her incessant recitation of the Koran.

Of her sayings, it is recorded:

"Ever since God gave me prevalence over the passions of my lower soul *(nafs)*, their fulfillment has ever been thwarted."

Sofyān Aiyana related that Omm Talq once reproached him, "How beautifully do you chant the Koran! I hope that this does not cause you distress on the Day of Judgment." Then she wept bitterly until she swooned.[1]

She also said, "Should you manage to restrain the passions of the lower soul *(nafs),* you shall be a sovereign; but if you follow its dictates, you will be a slave" (Ebn Jāwzi, *Şefat aş-şafwat)*

OMM ADAB

Dho'n-Nun Meşri (d. 861) cites Omm Adab as being among the devout and holy women of her time. She lived to ninety years of age. Every year, while performing the ceremonial duties of the Muslim pilgrimage, she walked on foot from Medina to Mecca.

Finally she lost her eyesight. When the season of the annual pilgrimage arrived that year, her women friends came to pay their respects and offer their condolences to her for her blindness. Weeping, she raised her head to the skies and uttered the following supplication, "Upon Your Glory, by Your Grandeur, if before Your Countenance my eye's vision has vanished, the light of my longing has not been extinguished." Binding her pilgrim's garb about her, she cried out "I come, O God! At Your service!"

Accompanied by a party of women devotees, she then set out towards the Ka'ba going even more quickly than her friends, out-pacing them all. Even Dho'n-Nun Meşri was surprised at her speed. Then a Divine voice chided him, "Why O Dho'n-Nun, are you amazed? How should not God's Mercy transport a woman who yearns to attain the House of her Lord?"

[1]*I.e.* The element of egotism found in your recitation veils your spritual development. (Trans.)

(Shaikh Sho'aid al-Ḥorayfish, *Al-Rawḍh al-fā'iq,* p. 117)

OMM MOḤAMMAD

Omm Moḥammad was a devout woman and the aunt of the well-known Sufi, Muḥyi'd-Din 'Abdo'l Qādir Gilāni (d. 1240). It is said that during a year-long drought in Gilān, prayers were offered up daily for rain, yet no rain fell. The population then went to Omm Moḥammad, imploring her to intercede with her prayers. Omm Moḥammad stood before her house and prayed, "O Lord, I swept my door-step, now You sprinkle the water"[1] Then she stayed outside the house in prayer until it began to pour. (Jāmi, *Nafaḥat al-ons)*

OMM MOḤAMMAD, MOTHER OF SHAIKH ABU 'ABDO'LLAH EBN KHAFIF

In the company of her son, Abu 'Abdo'llāh Ebn Khafif (d.1000), Omm Moḥammad travelled by sea to southern Arabia. Many visions *(mokāshafāt)* are ascribed to her, and she engaged in much spiritual struggle *(mojāhedā).*

It is related that in the last third of the month of Ramadan, Shaikh Khafif maintained the night vigil in order to discover which night was the renowned 'Night of Power'*(Laylo'l-qadr).* For this purpose, he climbed on the roof and began to perform the night prayers. His mother remained in the house, engaged in her own

[1]It is an Iranian custom to sprinkle water when sweeping, to settle the dust. (ed.).

spiritual meditation. Suddenly, the revelation of the lights of the "Night of Power" overcame her. "O Moḥammad, my son," she exclaimed, "what you seek for above, I have found down here."

Coming down from the roof, Shaikh Khafif also perceived those lights and fell prostrate at the feet of his mother. He confessed, "I knew, from then on, the true worth of my mother." (Jāmi, *Nafaḥāt al-ons)*

OMM HARUN

According to the account of 'Abdo'l 'Aziz Ebn 'Amir, "Omm Hārun was a pious lady of a God-fearing nature who was content with eating only bread. She would often say, 'I have assessed the world such as it truly is.'

She also said, 'How lovely, how pure is the night. I labor all day long, only for the sake of night's arrival. I rise to pray at sunset, and when dawn breaks, find that my heart has opened.' "

Qāsem Ju'i tells the following story about her:

> Once Omm Hārun fell sick and I went to pay her a visit along with one of my friends. When we entered the room we found her perched on top of a ladder. After asking after her health, I questioned her, saying 'Omm Hārun, are there any slaves of God whose fear of hell-fire is so intense that they are hindered from yearning for Heaven?'
>
> Upon hearing my question, she sighed, then swooned off the ladder onto the ground.

Aḥmad Ebn Abi al-Ḥawāri[1] (d. 845) related the following tale about Omm Hārun:

> Omm Hārun left her village one day with a certain destination in mind. On the way, she encountered some children playing. One boy said to the other, 'Hey, grab her!' [Hearing this as a Divine admonition] Omm Hārun fell to the ground, her head striking a stone, so that blood appeared on her scarf.
>
> Abu Sulayman Dārani remarked, 'Whoever wishes to see what is really meant by 'swooning', he would just have to look at Omm Harun'. adding, 'The like of her cannot be seen throughout all of Syria.'

Qāsem Ju'i has also related the following account:

> Omm Hārun walked on foot every month from Damascus to Jerusalem. Once, while I visited her, she said, "I passed by Baysān once and encountered a wild dog which came at me. I took one look at it and said, 'Dear dog, if I am your daily bread, you are welcome to eat me.' But as soon as I spoke those words, the dog retreated and ran away.

Aḥmad Ḥawāri once asked Omm Hārun whether she looked forward to dying. She replied, "No," and he wondered about her answer. She then declared, "When one disobeys a human being, any subsequent encounter with him is distasteful. How then can I expect to enjoy encountering God after so much

[1] One of the most eminent Syrian masters and a student of Abu Sulaimān Dārāni (d. 830).

disobedience?" (Ebn Jawzi, *Şefat aş-şafwat)*

BIBIAK OF MARV

The great Shaikh Abu Sa'id Abo'l-Khair has written:

> During the time we dwelled in Marv, there was an elderly lady name Bibiak who once came to us with a complaint, "Ordinary and common people pray to God in order not to be abandoned, even for one breath, to their egos. Yet I, for thirty years, have been invoking God and praying that for only the space of a wink of an eye, I might return to myself in order to see who I am or whether I still exist at all. But still, I have not found such an opportunity." (Jāmi, *Nafaḥāt al-ons)*

BIBICHEH KHALVATI

Bibicheh Khalvati (the Recluse) was a woman totally dominated by spiritual sentiments. She lived during the era of Jahānshāh Qarāqoyonlu.[1] Her grave is located near Sorkhāb in Tabriz. (*Rawḍhāt al-janān.* Vol I, p.222)

[1]Jahānshāh became the Shah of Azerbaijan in 1438 (ed.).

BARDAH-YE ŞARIMIYAH

Bardah-ye Şarimiyah was one of those devout women of Basra who possessed a gnostic (*'aref)* inclination. She was once asked how she had passes the day and replied, "Upon this earth of lonely exile, we are mere guests, waiting in expectation for a response from our Host."

Bardah-ye wept so abundantly that finally she could no longer see clearly. "God is distressed with you for this," people admonished her. "Don't you fear that you will lose your eyesight?" But Bardah-ye answered, "Let me be. If I am supposed to reside in hell, let God estrange me from Himself and seize my eyesight. But if I belong among the denizens of heaven, God shall restore to me a vision superior to this eyesight."

According to 'Atā Ebn Mobārak's account, Şarimiyah was venerated for her piety and sleeplessness:

> When the daily jobs were over and sleep overcame everyone, Şarimiyah would stand and sorrowfully supplicate, 'All eyes lie shut, the stars are setting, sweethearts have secluded themselves with each other—but Beloved, now we are alone together just You and me. When Your love fills my heart, shall You ever chastise me by hell-fire? O Love, never, never do this.' (Ebn Jawzi, *Şefat aş-şafwat)*

BAḤRIYA 'ABEDAH

Baḥriya 'Abedah was one of the pious devotees of Basra and a close associate of Shaqiq Balkhi (d. 809). Rabāh Ebn Abi al-Jarāḥ tells how he once saw Baḥriya weeping and confessing, "O Lord, I abandoned You in my youth, but now that I am an old woman, I have turned towards You. Accept this old woman as she is, with the slight beauty and grace she has, now that hunger has withered her." According to his account, in one period of forty days, she only ate a few chickpeas.

Baḥriya conducted religious assemblies and was educated as a jurisprudent *(mojtahed).* Whenever she lectured, she would become agitated and begin to tremble.

On the word of an old woman of Basra, Aḥmad Ebn Abi al-Ḥawāri has related the following saying of Baḥriya, "Whenever the heart abandons its passions, it becomes intimate with knowledge *('elm)*, and in its pursuit, endures patiently everything that occurs." (Ebn Jawzi, *Şefat aş-şafwat*)

BAIḌHA, DAUGHTER OF MOFAḌHḌHAL

Baiḍhā was a pious devotee who lived in Damascus. According to Aḥmad Ḥawāri's account, Asmā' Ramliya, a devout lady, once asked Baiḍhā, "O sister, are there certain indications by which a friend of God can be distinguished?" Baiḍhā replied, "Sister, is the lover ever concealed from his Lord? God's lovers cannot hide themselves, no matter how hard they try."

The woman beseeched her to elaborate further their characteristics. She responded, "If ever you see a lover, you have beheld something very strange indeed, for the lover has no place of rest throughout the whole earth. The lover is like a frightened bird, who feels most intimate in solitude, and flees from comfort. When hungry, his sustenance is love *('eshq);* when thirsty, his drink is love, and he is never depressed about the lengthy duration of his service to God." (Ebn Jawzi, *Şefat aş-şafwat*).

BARAKAH 'ABEDAH

Barakah 'Abedah was from Yamāmah in Arabia. There exists an account of her by Moslem Ebn Yasār, who visited Yamāmah as a trader. He relates:

> When I arrived in Yamāmah, all the people seemed to be converging on a certain house. Following them I entered the house and observed a woman adorned in rich and heavy clothes, who seemed to be aggrieved. She spoke little. All the residents of the house I saw there were either her slaves, servants or children. Men occupied in various business affairs—buying and selling different wares—passed in and out of her house.
>
> Having finished my business, sold my goods, and completed my travels, I returned to the house on another trip to bid everyone there farewell. None of the people whom I had previously seen in the house, however, seemed to be present when I entered—only the loud voice of a woman and her cackling laughter could be heard. I beheld a woman attired in charming, stylish clothes, seated in a fashionable room. I looked and saw that this laughter and mode of speech belonged to the same woman whom previously I

had noticed there, so I admonished her, 'What two strange states I have seen you in—one the other day, and one today!'

Upon hearing this, she rejoined, 'O Moslem, do not be surprised at me. As I was before, all I could see was prosperity and the abundance of leisure and wealth. No misfortune as yet had afflicted my soul or touched my children or finances. All my businesses were profitable and successful; my capital always on the increase, never lessening. Yet I still had this fear that my revenue would be nothing for me before God. So I grieved, thinking that if God really desired my welfare, He would have blighted my property and children. Now, at last, neither children nor wealth remain to me. Yet all of this only delights me; I suspect that God desires my well-being by way of these tribulations and this is His way of remembering me, and making my soul pure.'

Moslem further writes, "Later on, I encountered 'Abdo'llāh Ebn 'Omar and related this tale to him. He commented on its similarity to the legend of Job, who endured God's afflictions with patience, since God favors the patient. (Ebn Jawzi, *Solwat al-aḥzān*)

TOHFAH

Tohfah was a minstrel and slave-girl who was a contemporary of Sari Saqaṭi (d. 857). She was an ecstatic, transported from self and senses through the love of the Truth *(ḥaqiqat)*. She knew neither sleep nor food—day and night she spent crying and moaning; so deeply affected was she by her state that it ultimately proved too intense for her master's household to handle, so they sent her to a madhouse. In the latter part of Jāmi's *Nafaḥāt al-ons,* the following story is related by Sari Saqaṭi about Tohfah:

> One night, seized by some strange disquietude and tormented by insomnia, contraction (*qabḍh*) enveloped my spiritual state. I was impeded in the performance of my normal night prayers (*tahajod),* and no matter which supplications I offered up, I was unable to sense any state of expansion (*basṭ)* within myself, and I passed the entire night under the dire influence of that state. At daybreak it still remained.
>
> After morning prayers, I left home running hither and thither, trying to appease my anxiety, but to no avail. I reflected that if I went to a graveyard or a hospital and meditated on the situation of the dead and the diseased, my heart's condition might be eased and through sympathy and concern for those who are truly miserable, check the effect of this state upon myself. My heart chose to visit a hospital.
>
> Upon arriving there, my heart expanded and my breast rejoiced. I reflected upon the various ailments of each patient, and as I was leaving, I happened to chance by the door of a certain sick-chamber. My eye was caught by a young handmaiden whose fresh and unfading beauty seemed remarkable. She was attired in lavish but pure clothes, while a pleasant perfume wafted towards me from her. Yet both her feet and hands were shackled in chains. Her eyes overflowed with tears as she looked at me, and she recited the following verses:

I am neither traitor nor thief;
I am guiltless, and have perpetrated no crime.
Do you enjoy binding my hands in chains
Behind my back?

My liver is aflame within,
Searing my insides,
Yet I vow, O Beloved, a firm pledge,
A true oath to You:
Though You dismember me and tear me
Limb from limb,
I will never cease to contemplate You.

When I inquired of the wardens of the hospital who this girl was and why she had been cast into chains, I was informed that she was a slave-girl who had gone mad and, upon the recommendation of her owner, had been sent to the hospital for treatment. As she heard the warden describe her state, tears seemed to catch in the girl's throat. She then uttered the following verses:

Men, I am not mad but drunk!
My heart is all awareness and clarity.
My sole sin, my only crime,
Was to unashamedly be His lover
And to be disgraced,
Enraptured by the love of the Friend
Whose doorway I shall never desert.

Your idea of virtue to me is depravity;
What you understand as corruption
Is, for me, well-being.
Whoever loves the Lord of Lords
Choosing Him for himself alone,
Is immaculate, beyond sin.

My eyes became filled with tears, and her words seared my heart. 'This weeping of yours,' responded Tohfah, 'comes only from your knowledge of God's qualities. How would it be if you truly had realization of Him such as real gnosis requires?'

Then she fell into a trance, unconscious in a daze, for an hour. On regaining consciousness, she heaved a cold sigh from the depths of her heart, then uttered the following verses:

I delighted in Union's garb
With which You clothe me;
You are my Lord, and Lord in truth, over all.
Stray desires all overran my heart,
Yet every impulse gathered within You
Together, the moment I beheld You.

Throats that choke are cleared with water,
But what of one who chokes on water?
My heart, over ancient sins and errors all my own
Ponders and sorrows,
While this body-bound soul
Is overwhelmed with pain.

My mind is surfeited with yearning;
My body fills with burning while
Within my heart's profoundest corners
Your love is closeted.

How often have I fled back to You,
Begging Your pardon!
O Master, O Lord, You who know
What lies within me!
To the crowd I have handed over

Its world and faith;
And I am preoccupied recalling You,
You who are my faith and world.

Having sought You with such unbending envy,
I am now hated and envied;
Yet since You became my Lord,
I am now mistress over all.

'O sister,' I asked upon hearing this, 'how did you recognize me?' She replied, 'Ever since I became acquainted with Him, there is nothing I am stranger to.' I then said, 'I hear you speak of love, but whom do you love?' In response she professed, 'I love that One who made me aware of His bounty, whose favors put me under obligation, who is near to hearts, who replies to those who are in need.'

'Who has imprisoned you here?' I asked. She replied, 'Envious people, who all conspired with one another!' Then she uttered a loud cry, such that I thought she was going to die, and fell senseless. Upon regaining consciousness, she began to sing these verses:

My heart, intoxicated by the subtle wine
of affection and love,
Again yearns for its loved one.
O, weep! Be free in your tear-shedding, your
crying.
On the Day of Estrangement
Many tears there are whose falling
is solely good;
So many eyes God causes to weep with fear,
anxious over Him,
Then relieves and soothes.

That slave who sins unwittingly
but weeps in rue,
Is still owned as a slave;
Though bewildered and horror-stricken,
Within his heart a brilliant lamp is lit.

At that I signalled to the head of the hospital to allow her to leave, and I bade her go wherever she wished.

'Where should I go?' she questioned. 'There exists no place I may go, and He who is my heart's dear Friend has indentured me as a slave to another of His slaves. I will go only if my master approves, else I will forbear.'

'By God,' I observed to myself, 'she is wiser than I.'

Tofah's master suddenly appeared at the hospital, quite unexpectedly, making inquiries concerning her condition. They notified him that she was inside, in the company of Shaikh Saqaṭi. He was delighted at this news and when announced, greeted me with great ceremony.

'Better you had paid your respects to this maiden before me,' I rebuked him. 'Why have you imprisoned her?'

'The girl is out of her mind' *('aql),*' he replied, 'and refuses to eat or drink or sleep. She is always pensive, weeps continally and allows no one else any sleep. All my wealth and capital I spent to buy her—twenty thousand dirhams altogether. I set my hopes on her, imagining her profit to me would be in proportion to the price I paid for her with all her skills and talents.'

'What skills does she have?' I pressed.

'She is a singer and a minstrel,' he replied.

'For how long has this ailment indisposed

her?' I inquired.

'For one year now,' he answered, 'this same condition has controlled her.' I asked as to its initial symptoms. He said, 'She was humming the following verses one day while seated beside a lute:

Your artifice and cunning
have ravished my heart a hundredfold.
How strict are all Your vows!
Though I have accompanied others be-times,
Never have I severed our pledge of friendship.

Mad desire for union with You
Inflames me, while my breast seethes with
passion.
Once You granted me my primal sustenance.
Now, why have You forsaken me, Beloved,
amongst men?
Why, at first, did You concern Yourself
With me, if ultimately, You wanted to imprison
me, slave-bound,
Captive to creatures?

O tell me what or who I am and why
With such slow torture You draw me
Towards You? This world's existence
Without You, is merely a penitentiary,
Whereas life with You, even in Hell,
Is a garden of delights.

Grief's darts have struck my heart!
From whence have Your manacles of
melancholy entrapped me?
How many arrows more
Upon my soul shall you loose?

Till when shall I stay locked in chains?
Bring on the chains!
The chains and fetters!
And then a cell
Of further heart-constriction!

Tofah's master continued, 'All at once, having strummed these verses, she seized her harp and hurled it to the ground, bursting out in tears. Everyone present assumed that she had fallen in love with someone.'

'What are all these tears', we asked, 'and with whom have you fallen in love?' Hoarsely and broken-heartedly, she then wailed these verses:

Reality spoke up to me,
Invoked me from inside.
Yet my answering supplication
was already planted within me.
Though forlorn and alien,
Again to intimacy He summoned me . . .
Submissively, I obeyed His summons,
Affirming my Caller's address.
I feared my former sins, still,
Remaining pensive and seared. . .
Till fear was transfigured to fortune.

'That was how she fell ill,' concluded Tohfah's master.

'Whatever her price was to you, I will pay it,' Shaikh Saqaṭi replied when he heard the story. 'Even more if you ask.'

Tohfah's master rejoined, 'O darvish, you are a *faqir*, a beggar. You could never afford her price.'

I told him not to be hasty and to wait until I

collected the cash and brought it back to him. Crying rivers of tears, I left the hospital. I swear to God, not even a single dirham of her price was in my possession at the time. All alone that night, unable to shut my eyes, I sought only to lower and humble myself before God, supplicating, 'Lord, You know my inner being and see my external self. Only in Your grace and bounty have I trusted, do not disgrace me now!'

Suddenly, I heard a knock at the door. I asked who was there. An unfamiliar voice answered, 'A friend.' When I opened the door, there stood a strange man, carrying a candle, followed by four slaves. 'Grant us leave to enter, O master,' the stranger begged, 'I have something to tell you.'

'Come right in,' I said. They entered, and I asked his name.

'Aḥmad Mosni,' he informed me.

'What is your business here?' I asked.

'A hidden voice (*hātef*),' he replied, 'bade me to take these five purses of gold to Sari Saqaṭi to cheer him that he may purchase Tohfah, for we wish to show our special favor toward him.'

Hearing this, I kissed the earth in gratitude and stayed awake, waiting until morning. Immediately after prayers, I took Aḥmad Mosni by the hand and together we set out for the hospital. We encountered the warden standing at the portal, glancing right and left. He expressed joy on seeing me.

'Welcome, be at ease,' he said, 'For Tohfah has high worth before God. Last night a secret voice communicated the following to me:

Surely We treasure her,
And she is never without Our grace;
She draws near to Us, ascends higher and higher,
Advancing toward Us in all her states.

We walked over to Tohfah's cell; as she saw us coming, she sang the following lines:

So profoundly have I suffered
These various degrees of patience
That now my tolerance is through;
My endurance of shackles and bonds is ended.
No more exams may I take in love's aching,
No more tests of bosom-pain...

You, You are my heart's sole profit,
Essence of all my yearning;
None of my deeds from You are shrouded.
Unbind these weighty shackles from my back
today!
Free me from the fetters of slavery!

Tohfah's eyes gazed at me and filled with tears. Then she muttered the following prayer, 'Lord, among people You have raised my repute.' She mused a moment, then with downcast head, confessed:

Why, O Lord, across the earth's surface
Have You lent me this worthless notoriety?
Was my inward life truly so meager
As to be excluded from the ranks
Of the unknown saints?
I claimed to be a stranger to all but You—
Too many men know me now.

While this was happening, Tohfah's master appeared, wailing and weeping. I enjoined him not to cry and said, 'The price you demanded I have brought—with five thousand dinars profit to boot.'

'By God, no,' he replied.

'But I'll give you ten thousand dinars extra,' I pressed.

'No, by God,' again he refused.

'I'll pay twice the price you purchased her for,' I continued.

'No, master,' he admitted. 'Were you to offer me the whole world for her, I still would not accept.'

His response bewildered me. 'Why will you not accept my offer?' I entreated.

Then he explained, 'I have freed Tohfah; she is absolutely free to follow God's will.'

I pressed him to elaborate.

'O teacher,' he began, 'last night I was rebuked by God, and I firmly swear, with you as my witness, that I have renounced all my wealth and have fled for refuge to God. O Lord, be my bail throughout life and be generous with my daily bread!'

When I glanced at Mosni, I saw that he too was weeping. 'Why are you crying?' I inquired.

'I sense that God is not satisfied with my fulfillment of His (previous) summons,' he said. 'I wish you to act as a witness that I have abandoned all my wealth as well.'

'How great a blessing (*barakat*) has Tohfah been for all of us,' I remarked.

Tohfah then stood up, threw off the fancy costume she was wearing, and attired herself in rough sackcloth. She at once set out, though she was still crying.

'O Tohfah,' I implored, 'God has set you free. You should be happy now, not tearful.'

From Him unto Him I have fled
And He is in truth my Lord.
I am always beside Him til fulfillment
Since the advantage for which I hope
Is in Him alone.

She then left. A little while later we all went out, but however much we searched for Tohfah, we couldn't find her.

She fled — trailing tears
Adorned in a frock of coarse, dark wool.
A moon beneath a cloud blazed forth
Then was concealed under the arches.

Time went by and, accompanied by Tohfah's master and Aḥmad Mosni, I set out on a pilgrimage to the Ka'ba. Aḥmad Mosni died enroute to Mecca. At last we attained to God's House and while performing the ritual circumambulation of the Ka'ba, I suddenly heard a strange mournful wail, a forlorn cry that seemed to echo from a tormented heart:

The lover of God in this world
Ails and sorrows with long-drawn pain,
While suffering is his very remedy.

Out of love, God proffers him a goblet;
Then quenches him too.
Towards Him, enraptured and drawn
The lover turns, desiring no other Beloved.

So it is, for the ravished one
Until he attains the Beatific Vision.

I was deeply affected by this poem and the mournful wail accompanying it. I approached the singer. In recognition, she exclaimed, 'Sari!'

'But who are you?' I begged.

'May God forgive you!' she replied. 'God be glorified; there is no deity besides Him. Once I was famous, now again, I am obscure. It is me, Tohfah.'

How long, O master, shall you pretend
not to know me?
Step up and look O teacher
so observant of the truth!
He saw a slave-girl prostrate nigh to death,
Her full-moon face waned to a crescent,
Her erect cypress-like stature crippled,
Her eyes weeping, bloody in anguish,
Her soul at lip's end,
Her heart suspended.
"O love, pure love how are you?" he begged.
"I am" she affirmed, "as God wills."

'O Tohfah,' I asked, 'what profit did you see in abandoning physical comfort and embracing calamity?'

She replied, 'God, the All-High, bestowed intimacy upon me, brought me close beside Him and made me fearful of all but Him.'

When I informed her that Mosni had passed away during our pilgrimage, she commented, 'In Paradise, he shall be my neighbor. No eye has ever seen the Grace which is to be rendered to him.'

I informed her that her former master had also travelled in our company. She offered up a brief prayer for him, then fell beside the Ka'ba and surrendered her soul. Tohfah's master appeared just then, and seeing her dead, fell in grief on the ground beside her. I glanced down, and he too had passed away.

My heart was consumed with anguish but I managed to wash, shroud and bury them both. Then I returned home.

Do not wonder at those slain
In the dust at the Friend's door
Marvel rather, how anyone can survive,
With soul intact!

TAHIYAH NAWBIYAH

Tahiyah was one of the saintly women of Egypt, posssessing a gnostic outlook. Solami, on the word of Mālini Sufi, relates the following story about her:

When I went to pay my respects to Tahiyah, I heard her making the following petition to God from within her house, 'O Thou who lovest me, I love Thee also!' After entering her house and greeting her, I asked 'Though you love God, Tahiyah, how do you know He loves you?'

She replied, 'I once lived in Nubia, where my parents were Christian. One day, my mother brought me to church and took me up to the foot of the cross and told me to kiss it. As I leaned forward to kiss the cross, I saw a hand stretch out and turn my head about so my lips couldn't touch it. From long past, I thus understood that God has protected me with a very special grace.' (Ebn Jawzi, *Şefat aş-şafwat*)

THAWBIYAH, DAUGHTER OF BOHLUL

"Thawbiyah, the daughter of Bohlul," related Ebn Abi al-Ḥawāri, "was one of the women ascetics of Damascus. She used to pray, 'Light of my eyes! Nothing in this world or the next affords me any pleasure unless You be with it. Do not ever unite separation from You together with Your chastisement.' "

(Ebn Jawzi, *Şefat aş-şafwat*)

ḤAFSAH

Ḥafsah was the sister of Moḥammad Sirin.[1] Like her brother she was renowned both for her charismatic graces (*karāmāt*)and as a symbol of austerity and asceticism. It is said that Ḥafsah could recite the entire Koran at the age of twelve.

'Aşem Aḥwal recounts the following story about her:

> Once we visited Ḥafsah. She was wearing her veil in such a manner as to shroud her entire body. We were taken aback and reproached her saying, "God have mercy on you. Do you not remember God's own pronouncement: 'Such elderly women as are past the prospect of marriage, there is no blame on them if they lay

[1]He was one of the followers (*tāba'in)* of the Prophet's companions, during the time of Ḥasan al-Basri.

aside their garments, provided they make no a wanton diplay of their beauty.' (Koran XXIV:60) 'The point of this precept,' I commented to her, 'is that you should cover yourself, not drape youself in the *chāddur.*'

Heshām Ebn Ḥasan has related that Ḥafsah would stay in the mosque all day performing her prayers and then spend all night in a position of genuflection (*roku'*) until sunrise. She would then take leave of the mosque, go home to renew her ablutions and refresh herself with sleep. When the time for ritual prayers came about again, she would return to the mosque and repeat the whole process.

According to Mahdi Ebn Maymun, Ḥafsah once spent three years upon her prayer carpet, only deserting it to satisfy nature or if someone summoned her.

According to Heshām, Ḥafsah's son possessed a female camel and every morning he would send his mother a cup of milk. Ḥafsah habitually told her son that she was fasting and unable to drink it. Her son, however, would reply, "Mother, the best milk is that which gathers overnight in the camel's udders. Take the cup and present it to whomever you like."

Ḥafsah once purchased a maidservant. Heshām relates that he thought the servant to be of Sindi origin. When he asked the servant what she thought of her mistress, however, she replied in Persian, "But for one grave sin, she is a very devout lady. In this she is guilty, that she wails and prays all night through."

'Abdo'l Karim Ebn Mo'āwiah has related that Ḥafsah used to recite the Koran every night and fast every day, except for the holidays of *'Id al-fetr,* at the end of the month of Ramadan, and the festival of sacrifice *('Id al-qorbān)* in the season of pilgrimage.

Ḥafsah used to wear her shroud *(kafan)* every time she made the pilgrimage to Mecca. She would also wear it while praying during the last nights of Ramadan.

"A certain light sometimes pervaded Ḥafsah's house during these times," relates Heshām. "At nightfall, Ḥafsah would light a lamp and stand to pray. Though her lamp sometimes went out, her house would remain illuminated till dawn." (Ebn Jawzi, *Ṣefat aṣ-ṣafwat*)

ḤABIBA 'ADAWIYAH

It is recounted that when Ḥabiba became absorbed in her devotion, she would often ascend to her roof and, dressed in her woolen frock and *chāddur*, supplicate:

> God! All the stars have set and all eyes are shut in sleep. Kings have shut their gates, yet Your portal is still open. Every friend has sought seclusion with his sweetheart, while I stand alone before Your face.

When dawn broke, she would pray:

> Night is behind us, day again has arrived. O, how I long to know whether this night has been worthy in Your eyes, so that I may be felicitous and applaud myself, or whether You have rejected my devotion so that I may console myself. By Your Magnificence I swear, such is

always my way of worship. I beg You inform me as long as I live, of my worthiness or Your disapprobation. If you cast me out, I swear I shall not leave Your doorstep, as nothing but Your grace and bounty can be contained in my heart. (Ebn Jawzi, *Ṣefat aṣ-ṣafwat*)

ḤALIMA OF DAMASCUS

Ḥalima was a descendant of the Prophet. She dwelled in Syria and was the teacher of Rābe'ah of Syria.

Rābe'ah, the wife of Aḥmad Ebn Abi al-Ḥawāri, once visited Ḥalima and has related the following story:

> When I entered, Ḥalima was reading from the Koran. She addressed me saying, 'Rābe'ah, I have heard that your husband desires another wife besides you.'
>
> 'Yes,' I affirmed.
>
> 'With all his intelligence, how can he allow his heart to become distracted from God with two wives? Have you not heard the interpretation of the Koranic verse 'But for one who comes towards God with pure heart. . .'?'[XXXVI:88-89]
>
> 'No,' I admitted.
>
> 'Its meaning,' she said 'is that you should attend to God, the Exalted, and not have anything other than Him in your heart.'
>
> As I left Ḥalima, I was so deeply moved by her words that I rocked back and forth as I walked in a kind of trance, but felt embarassed at my condition—that passersby might think me drunk. (Jāmi, *Nafaḥat al-ons*)

ḤAKIMA

Ḥakima was a member of the Bani Makhzum tribe who dwelled in the suburbs of Mecca. It was her custom to sit with her eyes fixed on the door of the House of the Ka'ba waiting for it to open, continually sobbing and wailing aloud until she swooned.

One day in her absence, the door of the Ka'ba was opened. After her arrival, onlookers described the panorama to her, "Ḥakima, God's House was open today! Could you have only beheld how the pilgrims were circumambulating the House with such a zeal, their hearts lacerated by yearning and intense longing, and how they were awaiting God's grace and pardon! Could you only have seen them abjectly weeping, begging for remission, you would have rejoiced."

Hearing this, Ḥakima shrieked as though her heart had been rent apart.

She was continually in a state of agitation, seeking Him whom she had lost in bewildered distraction. She lived pining to reach her goal, in constant longing tobehold the Ka'ba, which pleased her more than anything else in the world until her death. (al-Ḥorayfish, *Op. cit*, and Ebn Jawzi, *Şefat aş-şafwat*)

ḤASANA 'ABEDAH

"Once I heard of a lady called Ḥasana," relates Moḥammad Ebn Qodām, "who abandoned the ephemeral pleasures of the world, occupying herself totally in devotional works. She spent her nights in prayer and her days fasting. She had no possessions in her house, and whenever she found herself thirsty she would walk to a nearby stream, cup her hands and drink. Being of beautiful appearance, she was encouraged by another woman to marry.

'If you bring me a man of ascetic temperament,' Ḥasanah replied, 'who will not divert me with the affairs of the world, I will consider it. Yet such a person, I think, will be hard to find. I swear by God it is not my nature to adore the world or to amuse and divert myself with its men. If I can find a man who fasts and encourages me to fast also, who cries and would stimulate me to weep as well, who gives alms and would stir me to be charitable as well, that is fine, and I am ready; otherwise, no.' " (Ebn Jawzi, *Ṣefat aṣ-ṣafwat*)

ḤAYYUNA

Rāshed Ebn 'Alqamah Ahwāzi relates the following prayer of Ḥayyuna which she habitually made at nightfall:

> O my Beloved, One and Unique! You hinder me at night from the recitation of the Koran, then in the daylight hours estrange Yourself from me. My God, if only my days could be night so that I might benefit from nearness to You.

Salām Aswad has recounted that Ḥayyuna was disturbed one day by the sun's rising and beseeched God, saying, "If You really know that I am Your lover, O Lord, take the scorching rays of the sun off my face."

Clouds at once covered the sky.

Salām has related that Ḥayyuna once fasted until she turned black and people began to criticize her. She lifted her head to heaven and implored, "When I try to serve You, Your creatures scoff at me. By Your majesty and glory I swear that I shall serve You till neither bones nor nerves remain in me."

She then intoned the following verse:

O You who vow good pleasure to Your friends,
Besides You I desire no one.

Once Rābe'ah of Syria went to visit Ḥayyuna and was overwhelmed by sleep in the middle of the night. Ḥayyuna arose and nudged her, "Rise up, it is the hour of the banquet of those who are rightly guided. It is by the efforts of your prayers that the brides of night are beautified."

Salām reports that Ḥayyuna once encountered 'Abdo'l Wāḥed and reprimanded him by saying "First admonish your own soul, O preacher. I swear by God, I shall not follow your bier after death."

"'Why not?" he inquired.

Ḥayyunah answered, "You converse with people and try to be close to them, just like a child who goes to his mother's house and forgets his lesson, so that reluctantly the teacher is obliged to punish him. Go, and scourge your own passion instead, 'Abdo'l Wāḥed: take stock in reliance upon God. First allow your own soul to profit by your sermons, then preach to others."

The words of Ḥayyuna caused 'Abdo'l Wāḥed to break out in a sweat, and he totally abandoned human company for a year.

Salām has also related that Ḥayyunah once said:

> Whoever loves God, will gain intimacy with Him. Whoever becomes joyous will become desirous. Whoever becomes desirous will become bewildered in love. Whoever becomes bewildered in love will become bold. Whoever becomes bold will reach Him. Whoever reaches Him will enter into Union. Whoever enters into Union will become a knower (*'āref*). Whoever becomes a knower will be drawn near. Whoever draws near will not fall asleep, and the rays of heartache engulf such a person.

Ḥayyuna is said to have continually supplicated, "O God, by the bond of trust I have in You, give me peace of heart. Placate all my thoughts with contentment in You. Do not allow my lot to be distanced from You, O desire of all who yearn."

Ebrāhim reports that Rayhāna once went to see Ḥayyuna. That night there was a rainstorm and Rayhānah became frightened. Ḥayyuna, however, laughed and scolded her saying, "Faltering one, if ever I were to feel that my heart holds some love besides Him, or some fear of other than Him, I should strike it with a knife." (Nayshāpūri, *Ketāb 'oqalā' al-majānin*, Vol. I, p. 407)

KHANSA, DAUGHTER OF KHADDAM

Khansā was one of the saints of Yemen, a lady free of attachments. According to the account of Ḥafṣ Ebn 'Amru Ja'fi, "She was a gentlewoman of Arabic descent, renowned for her beauty and lovely stature. She was called Khansā, the daughter of Khaddām. She maintained a fast for forty years, until finally her skin shrunk to her bones. She wept so excessively that finally she lost her eyesight, and she spent so many sleepless nights engaged in prayer that she was rendered unable to stand. Both Ṭāwus and Wahb Ebn Monyah had a very high regard for her station.

At night when all eyes were closed fast in sleep, and all activity had ceased, Khansā would lament in the following fashion:

> O Friend to those whose wills are resigned, how long shall You imprison Your faithful servants on earth? Quicken them until they behold the reality of Your pledges, for whose sake their souls are anguished and for which they toil. (Nayshāpūri, *Ketāb 'oqalā' al-majānin,*)

RABE'AH

Rābe'ah was the daughter of Shaikh Abu Bakr Bokhāri and the wife of Seyyed Aḥmad. She was a lady of great learning and spiritual insight. In addition to her many praiseworthy qualities, she was also a gnostic of high standing. Although called by her husband, "mother of the dervishes" (*omm al-foqarā*), she was generally known as "mistress of the dervishes" (*sett al-foqarā*). The state of fear of God (*khawf*) constantly enveloped her. She passed her life grieving and sorrowful, dying in 613 / 1216. (*Reyhānat al-adab*, Vol. 2, p. 439)

RAHMAT 'ABEDAH

Rahmat 'Abedah's state, it is said, was predisposed toward spiritual struggle *(mojāheda)*. When exhorted by people to be more merciful on her soul, to be easier on herself, she would respond, "Now is the time to advance upon it and despoil it. I swear by God that I am constantly engaged in prayer, throughout all my life's days, and shall weep as long as I have tears." (Ebn Jawzi, *Solwat al-aḥzān*)

ROQIYA

Roqiya was one of the gnostics and lovers of God from Mosul. 'Obayo'llāh Ebn 'Omar Ebn Mo'ammari recounts that his father told him the following saying of hers on the world of a Sufi from Mosul:

> O God, O Creator, though You inflict me with torment, it is nothing in comparison with what I lose from being far from You. Though with heaven's bounty You bless me, it is still less than the rapture with which Your love has favored my

heart.

Manṣur Ebn Moḥammad cites Roqiya as saying, "I so fervently love my Creator that if He summoned me to the fire, love of Him would not let me sense the heat. If He beckoned me to paradise, His love would bar me from finding any delight there, since His love has taken total possession of me."

Moḥammad Ebn Kathir Maṣiṣi relates that Roqiya once declared, "Anyone who sets his heart on monasticism for the sake of pleasing his fellow man is excluded from relishing the sweetness of faith. People occupy their hearts with the world instead of God. Were they only to abandon the world, their hearts would take wing in the World of Angels *(malakut)*, and they would profit greatly."

Roqiya has also stated, "Try to be learned concerning the right modes of devotional sincerity *(ekhlāṣ)*. Do not endeavor to gain knowledge of that which will draw you hither and thither." (Ebn Jawzi, *Ṣefat aṣ-ṣafwat*)

ROQIYA, DAUGHTER OF DA'UD SAMMADI

The Master Sarrāj narrates that a group of his comrades communicated to him that Shaikh Dā'ud had a daughter called Sayyedah Roqiya. One evening this same company gathered in Dā'ud's house to listen to one of the special concerts (*samā'*) of the Sufis. Roqiya stood in the doorway of the room in which they were assembled, concentrating on the gathering. At the conclusion of the *samā'*) she suddenly told all of the Sufis to leave the room quickly. As soon as they had exited, the entire floor and rug on which they had been assembled collapsed.

Roqiya then declared, "Certain men attempted to ruin my concentration. I prevented them as much as possible, but neglected to keep my attention on the floor under your feet. They ruined it from beneath, but I maintained the carpet on which you were dancing, suspended in midair by the grace and power of the Almighty, till morning." (Nabahāni, *Jāme' al-karāmat al-auliyā'*)

REYHĀNA, THE GOD-INFATUATED (*WALEH*)

Reyhāna was one of the devout ladies of Basra who lived during the time of Sāleḥ Meri (d. 790). She wore these verses in a locket, suspended from her neck:

O You, my Friend, my ecstasy and aspiration,
Besides You, my heart spurns all other love.
O Beloved, my long-enduring ambition and
yearning is to behold You.
Among all the pleasures of Paradise
Only union with You do I wish.

(Ebn Jawzi, *Ṣefat aṣ-ṣafwat*)

PRINCESS ZOBAYDA

Zobayda was the daughter of Fatḥ 'Ali Shāh Qajar, who ruled Iran from 1797 to 1834. She was a mystic and a poetess, in addition to possessing numerous laudable virtues. She devotedly observed the precepts of her religion and sponsored the establishment of many charitable institutions. She also provided funds for the repair of numerous shrines. Her pen-name was Jahān, and she left behind a *Divan* of verses of which the following lines are an example:

How lovely, how sweet they murmured
within my heart's inward ear,
Are you a lover? Then go crazy, crazy!
If Union you desire,
and consummation with Him you crave,
then to your ego be alien.

If to Love you are true, and to Him sincere,
Then burn your ego, consume your self.
Soar into love's blaze like a moth
Be a moth, O heart, a moth.

Come Cupbearer!
Bring me a glass or two of wine,
So that a few drunken verses I may utter
Burning in my inner anguish.
In this drunkenness and intoxication
I will drive all memory of self into oblivion.

Other than You will not remain,
Only you ever subsistent
Love-sick and bewildered

The whole world wanders crazed
Over the Beloved's face.
Only a crazy lover talks this way,
Drunken in a stupor.

Zobayda was a disciple of Hājj Mirzā 'Ali-Naqi Hamadāni. She was assiduous in the performance of her religious duties, and virtually all of her leisure time was occupied with litanies and prayers.

Zobayda travelled on twenty different occasions to the Shrines of the Shi'ite Imams in Iraq, and also performed pilgrimage to Mecca and Medina. In addition, she went to Mashad ten times as a pilgrim to the sanctuary of Imam Reza (the 8th Shi'ite Imam). When travelling Zobayda never brought any articles of luxury along, yet her generosity toward others was seemingly inexhaustible, such that all classes of Persian and Arabic society benefitted from her benevolence.

Zobayda married 'Ali Khān Noṣrat al-Molk, the son of Rostam Khan Qaraqozlu. They had a child named Ḥosayn. At the time she composed the *Khayrāt Hesān* (1304/1887), Zobayda was eighty years old.

It is said that few people were so widely respected and acclaimed for their piety in their day as she was. (*Rayḥānato'l-adab,* II p. 361.)

ZOJLAH 'ABEDAH

Zojlah was originally from Basra; she had been a slave of the Caliph Mo'āwiya, but was eventually freed by him.

Aḥmed Ebn Sahl Azdi describes his meeting with Zojlah as follows:

> Zojlah constantly recited the Koran. When I visited her, I entreated her to exercise more mercy upon herself. She replied, 'I can't feel any mercy towards myself, and now is the very time to proceed against the self, for whatever I omit today, tomorrow I shall be unable to regain. For God's sake, O brother, I swear that so long as my limbs avail me, I shall pray and fast for Him, and as long as my eyes hold tears I shall weep for Him.' As an after-thought, Zojlah added, 'Which of you would command someone to do something imperfectly?'
>
> Abu 'Otbah Khawāss narrates that when he visited Zojlah her skin had turned black from fasting, excessive weeping had caused her to lose her vision, and her immoderate amount of praying had made her unable to stand up, forcing her to pray kneeling.
>
> He endeavored to speak to her of God's forgiveness and pardon, wishing to lighten her load. Stifling her tears, Zojlah answered, 'What I know of my own lower soul *(nafs)* so galls my heart that I truly wish, by God, that He had not created me and that I had never been anything worthy of mention.'
>
> Kalib Ebn 'Isā Abi Hajir recounts that Zojlah never lifted her eyes to heaven and spent her days washing people's clothing at the river bank.
>
> Sa'id Ebn 'Abdo'l-'Aziz considered Zojlah the

most learned person in Syria and Iraq. (Ebn Jawzi, *Şefat aş-şafwat*)

ZAHRA, THE GOD-INTOXICATED (*WALEHAH*)

According to Moḥammad Ebn Salameh, Dho'n-Nun Meşri has related the following description of his encounter with Zahrā Wālehah:

> Once I was wandering through a rough mountain valley outside Jerusalem when I heard someone making the following supplication, 'O gracious Lord, Your bounties are too many to be enumerated. O generous Lord, possessor of everlastingness, may my heart's eye be blessed to view Your bounty's garden. O Subtle One, allow me to rest at one with Your mercy and munificence. O Kind One, give me a share of the ways of those bewildered in You by Your splendor and light. Make me pursue You unceasingly and serve You unwaveringly. O Light-bestower of my heart, goal of my quest, befriend me in Your wiṣdom.'
>
> On pursuing the sound of the voice, I perceived a woman as thin as a stick of incense. She wore woolen clothing and a veil woven of hair. She had striven in spiritual warfare and grief had slain her. Love had melted her and ecstasy had annihilated her.
>
> 'Salām,' I greeted her.
>
> 'Peace be upon you, O 'Dho'n-Nun,' she replied. 'There is no god but Allah!' I exclaimed.

'How do you know my name, if you never saw me before?'

'In my innermost conciousness,' she rejoined, 'my Beloved disclosed your name to me, and rent aside the veil of blindness which beclouded my heart, so I became aware of your name.'

'Return to your prayers, ' I begged her.

'O Light-giver,' she supplicated, 'enable me to distance myself from the evil of what I behold, for I am alienated from all life.' She then fell upon the ground dead. I remained there bewildered, sunk in meditation. Suddenly there came an old woman whose features were similar to those of Zahrā Wālehah. Staring at the corpse, she exclaimed, 'Thank God, He showed His generosity to her.'

'Who is she?' I asked.

'Haven't you heard of Zahrā Wālehah?' she asked. 'She is my daughter. For twenty years now everyone has thought her insane. She was slain by longing for God.' (Ebn Jawzi, *Ṣefat aṣ-ṣafwat*)

ZAYTUNA

Zaytuna, or Fāṭema, was an associate of Abu Ḥamza, Jonaid and Nuri. (God sanctify their spirits!) She recounted the following story about Nuri:

> On a severely cold day, I called upon Nuri, asking if there was anything he wanted to eat.
>
> 'Yes,' he answered.

'What can I bring you?' I asked.

'Bread and milk,' he answered.

When I brought them before him, he was sitting beside a fire, his hand charred black by contact with the ashes. I noticed that as he dipped his fingers in the bread and milk, half his hand was washed white by the milk, while the rest of his hand was still coal black. I thought to myself, 'Lord, how dirty are Your friends. There's no one clean person among them.'

Rising I left his presence, and on my way a woman stopped me, saying, 'I left a sack of clothes here. You stole it.' She then brought me before the governor.

Nuri, in the meantime, had gotten word of my case, and followed after me. 'She is of the saints of God,' he pleaded. 'Don't hurt her.'

'Fine,' replied the governor, 'but what ruse can I use to get this person off her back?'

At that moment, a slave presented himself with the missing bundle in hand. 'Free her,' the governor directed, 'I've found the article.'

Nuri took me by the hand away from the governor. He asked me, 'Why did you say , "How frightening and dirty are Your friends"?'

I replied, 'I repent of my statement.' (Jāmi, *Nafaḥāt al-ons*)

ZAYNAB

Zaynab, the daughter of Abu Barakāt, was from Baghdad. She was a pious lady, endowed with many talents and virtues. She often preached to her fellow women and gave instructions to them in jurisprudence and literature as well. A special *khaniqah* (Sufi house), named the *Rebāt al-Baghdādiya,* was built in her honor by Malek Zāher, the Sultan of Egypt. Zaynab lived in the latter half of the sixth century A.H., and the early part of the seventh century. (*Rayḥanat al-ādab*, Vol. 6, p. 360)

LADY SAKINA SHIRAZ

Sakina Begum (Lady Sakina) was the daughter of Mirzā 'Abdo'llāh and came from a family in Shiraz which was descended from the Prophet. The pen-name she employed for most of her poetic works was *'Effat* (the Pure One). She can be considered one of the outstanding women of the early nineteenth century with gnostic understanding. Below are a few selections of her verse, translated from the Persian:

Moon-faced, my Saqi carries,
Two ruby-shaded chalices of wine in hand;
From His lips two kisses I steal,
From His palm two flasks.

O, my inner state and my Beloved
Are as one soul cast into two bodies.
How fantastic this fleshly difference,
One individual called by two names!

Your tresses, hanging from either side,
Snare the bird of my heart.
How hard it is to accept

از روی انکار می گفته اند که این صورت مناسب نیست که حضرت شیخ از کتاب می کنند آن
درویش این سخن را در مجلس آنحضرت مذکور ساخته بزبان شیراز فرموده یکیش وا رزه و نواز
خوشش یکیش وا چرخ و باز خوش پیکین ور زبهان کش وا یکی سرو ناز خوش یکنوبت در شهر

شیراز جوان بخدمت شیخ مشغول بود و پای آنحضرت را می مالید چنانکه شیخ عراقی فرماید

چون با بویان عاشقی بر شد روز به بود روز بهتر شد سالها با جمال جان افروز

2

Shaikh Ruzbehan Baqli preaching to a gathering of male and female disciples. From the *Majāles al-'oshshāq* (dated 1552) in the Shirazi Style. Oxford Bodleian Library Ms. Ouseley Add.24 (Ethé 1271), f. 54a.

A single prey caught in two snares!

I have come here to discourse on Love:
Myself, a soldier, and a Mulla
Yet how can I respond to them?
One of us is well-done, while two are half-baked.

These lines are also by her:

Did the curls of those scattered locks
Learn from the hyacinth?
Or did the hyacinth learn its curls
From those locks?

Did I learn to cry and weep
From the songbird?
Or did the songbird learn its singing
From me?

(*Tarā'eq al-haqā'eq*. III, p. 235)

LADY MOLUK

Shaikh Ṣafi ad-Din Ebn Abi Manṣur recounts that he saw a great lady who was one of God's saints. She was called Lady Moluk, highly esteemed by the men of knowledge in the Maghreb.

Once she went on a pilgrimage to Jerusalem. An outstanding shaikh named 'Ali Ebn 'Isā Yamāni, was there, and gives the following account:

Once when I was in Jerusalem I saw strands of light stretching down from heaven to the dome of the mosque. I set out for the dome, and when I arrived I saw Lady Moluk. The light I had seen was connected to her. I requested that she accept me as her brother, and she agreed. (Nabuhāni, *Karāmat al-auliya'*)

SA'IDAH ṢUFIYAH

She was one of the recluses of this way and is mentioned by Solami in *Tabaqāt al-nāsekāt.* A group of Sufis, wanting to greet her and gain her blessing, went to the door of her cell and said, "Recite a prayer for us." She replied, "May God cut off from you everything that cuts you off from Him." (*Asrār al-tawhid,* p. 326)

SALMŪNA

Sahl Ebn Sa'd relates that there was a woman named Salmūna in Abādān who was enraptured, mad in love of God. During the day she would conceal herself so that no one would see her. At night she would go up to the roof of her house and supplicate until dawn, crying, "My Lord and my Master! You have separated me from my reason, made me terrified of Your creatures and intimate with Your remembrance (*dhekr).* Your creatures have driven me away. Woe upon me if You also drive me away!"

(Nishapuri, *Ketāb al-'oqalā' al-majānin)*

SHA'WANA

She was a Persian who lived in Obollah on the Tigris. She had a good voice and used to preach and recite in a beautiful chant. Ascetics, men of piety, and Sufis used to attend these sessions.

Among her sayings was that it is improper for an eye that is prevented from seeing its Beloved and desirous of doing so, to be without tears. It is related that when afflicted by spiritual desolation, her performance of prayers and devotions was inhibited. Falling asleep, someone in a dream recited these verses to her:

Spill tears if you have grief
As tears of grief provide relief.
Strive to be straight
Try to be upright upon the Path
To fast and heave sighs of burning grief.
For the way of those acquiescent to God
Is to live with sighs and burning grief.

Rising up, she resumed her devotion, weeping and humming the verses to herself. Other woman wept with her.

They say that when she became old, Foḍhail Ebn 'Iyāḍh came to see her and asked her to pray for him. She replied, "Is there anything between you and God that makes you think he would answer?" At that he cried out and fainted.[1]

Mo'ādh Ebn Fazl relates, "Sha'wāna cried so much that we thought she would go blind. When I mentioned this to her, she said, 'By God, it is better for me to go blind in this world because of tears, than in *that* world because of fire."

Mālek Ebn Ḍhaigham related how a certain man from Oballah used to visit his father, Abu Kathir describing Sha'wana's condition and continual weeping. Upon being asked for more details, he replied: "Should I explain how she weeps night and day without any break?"

Mālek replied, "No, tell me how she begins to weep."

He said, 'When she hears any mention of God, tears begin to flow from within her like a rain."

Mālek asked, "Do the tears come mainly from the corner of the eye near the nose or from the corner near the temple?"

He replied, "Her tears are so abundant that I can not say from where they flow. I can only say that when the Name of God is mentioned, her eyes beome like four shining stars." Abu Kathir began to weep and said, "Her fear of God derives from the fact that the whole of her heart is on fire. They say that the amount a person weeps depends on the amount of fire in the heart."

---

[1]The above sections are from Jāmi, *Nafaḥāt al-ons.*

Mālek Ebn Zaygham relates that one day, his father went with Manbuḍh and Abu Homān to visit her in Oballah. Manbuḍh greeted her and told her he was the son of her brother. She replied, "Greetings to a nephew whom I have never before seen, but whom I love. By God, I would like to visit your father, but I do not, because I fear I might prevent him from worship. Serving God is much more necessary than he should talk with Sha'wāna. Who is she but a destitute and disobedient woman?" Then she began to weep and kept on weeping until we left.

Qorashi said, "I went with a friend to Oballah. We asked Sha'wāna's permission to visit with her. After admitting us into a poor cottage in which destitution was visible everywhere, my friend said to Sha'wāna, "O, if you only could have more compassion on yourself and lessen your crying, in the long run it would be better for you in obtaining the object of your desire."

Sha'wāna broke out crying again, and confessed, "I swear by God, I would like to cry until no tears are left. Such a shower of blood then I would weep, that no drop of blood would remain in any part of my body."

"My friend," cites Qorashi, "only reiterated his former request to Sha'wāna, yet her eyes turned back in their sockets and wept blood until she swooned and fell, whereupon we rose and left, leaving her as she was."

On the word of Ruḥ Ebn Salama, a certain Moḥammad quotes Moḍher as saying, "I never saw anyone weep as much as Sha'wāna, nor did I ever hear a voice similar to hers, scorching the hearts of those fearful of God. She would continually lament, "O dead one, O dead son, O dead brother!"

"I asked Abu 'Omar Ḍharir," recounted Moḥammad, "if he had ever encountered Sha'wāna."

"Yes," he admitted, "I have often frequented her gatherings, but she was so drowned in weeping that I could never fathom her sermons."

"Do you remember anything at all of what she said?"

"I can recall nothing," he said, "of her words, except the following declaration, 'Whosoever is present here and can weep, should do so, and if not, should pity the tears of others. For whoever cries here, does so from awareness of the full extent to which his lower soul (*nafs)* has crossed and confounded him, and understanding how his passions have made him a transgressor!' "

Of the verses of spiritual requiem that Sha'wāna would sing for her lady companions, the following are recorded:

To remain forever in the world you love
is an ambition beyond reach;
Remember the date-palm that still stands
after the gardener's demise.

Sha'wāna would often come to visit Ḥasan Ebn Yaḥyā Qorashi. He recounts, "She cried and stimulated others to tears as well. She would lament and cry out the following verse:

Secure he stands,
the proud man
upon his own,
within his home;

yet all this complacrnt peace shall pass
—indeed a day is near—
all the same it all shall change
to fright and fear

(Ebn Jawzi, *Ṣefat aṣ-ṣafwat*)

Sha'wāna went one year with her spouse on a pilgrimage. As they completed their circumambulation of the Black Stone, he exclaimed to his wife, "I so thirst for God's love that my tongue has left me."

"Diverse pains," Sha'wāna answered, "have diverse remedies. The remedy for the lovers of God is His Grace." (Ebn Jawzi, *Salwat al-aḥzan*)

Sha'wāna has further said, "Lord, You know that one who thirsts for Your love can never be sated."

One of Sha'wāna's devoted disciples stated that from the instant she laid eyes upon her, by way of the saint's charismatic blessing, never again did she feel inclined to pursue the world and never again did she feel contempt for a fellow Muslim. (Sha'rani, *Ṭabaqāt al-kobrā*, Vol. I, p. 51)

It is related that God gave Sha'wāna a son whom she raised with the best possible education. On reaching maturity, he begged his mother to allow him to dedicate his life to God. "It would improper to direct you toward kings and nobles, O son," his mother replied. "Better you keep the company of literary people and persons of good character. What's more, O son, you have not even tasted youth; you lack all conception of the demands which will be made of you and which will seem intolerable."

Her son held his silence. One day he set out for the mountains to chop wood and gather it for his mother. Reaching the middle slope of the mountain, he descended from his horse and engaged in his work, arranging each group of logs in a separate bundle. Upon finishing his work, he went to look for his horse to fasten the bundles on its back. In the meantime, however, a wild lion had attacked and broken the neck of his horse. The lion stood nearby. When Sha'wānah's son saw what had happened, he extended his arm and laid his hand on the beast's neck. Then he said, "In the same way that you have afflicted my horse, O rapacious beast, I shall, by God, burden you with this load of wood." Placing the firewood on the lion's back and the bit in his mouth, he led the animal to the gate of his mother's cottage and knocked on her door.

"Who is there?" she demanded.

"Your son is here," he answered, "begging for the mercy of God who is the Provider to all His devotees."

Opening the door, she beheld the firewood, bound to the back of the lion. "What is all this?" she inquired. As her son related the tale, his mother inwardly rejoiced, knowing that God had bestowed special grace upon him and had accepted him as a devotee.

"Now son," Sha'wāna replied, "you are worthy to wait upon kings. Go! I dedicate and entrust you to God." So she bade her son farewell, praying for his journey. (Nabahāni, *Jāme' Karāmāt al-āuliyā'*)

According to Dārā Shekuh's *Safinat al-auliyā'*, Sha'wāna died in 792.

SHAMS, MOTHER OF THE POOR

Among the eminent Sufis of the day, the name of Shams, Omm al-Foqarā' ('Mother of the Poor), should certainly be mentioned. Ebn 'Arabi describes his encounter with her when she was in her eighties in his autobiographical tract, *Resālat al-qods*, as follows:

> She lived at Marchena of the Olives where I visited her often. Among people of our kind I have never met one like her with respect to the control she had over her soul. In her spiritual activities and communications she was among the greatest. She had a strong and pure heart, a noble spiritual power and a fine discrimination. She usually concealed her spiritual state, although she would often reveal something of it to me in secret because she knew of my own attainment, which gladdened me. She was endowed with many graces. I had considerable experience of her intuition and found her to be a master in this sphere. Her spiritual state was characterized chiefly by her fear of God and His good pleasure in her, the combination of the two at the same time in one person being extremely rare among us.[1]

[1]Translated by R. W. J. Austin, *Sufis of Andalusia* (London, 1971) p. 142.

3

A male and female Sufi visiting with two female Sufis. Seventh century Mughal. B.M. 1920-9-17-010 (35) f.68.

'AISHA, IMAM JA'FAR AṢ-ṢADEQ'S DAUGHTER

'Aisha was sincerely dedicated to the way of devotion and love of God. Her faith in God's promise of succour and reward for good deeds was perfect. Hope prevailed over fear in her spiritual state. It is reported that 'Aisha, with all the confidence of her pure faith and trust in his bounty, would often address God as follows:

> By Your magnificence and majesty, I swear that if You hurl me into the inferno I will clutch my faith in Unity (*tawḥid)* and parade before the fire-dwellers, exclaiming, 'I have been subjected to this torment, though I recognized there is only one God.'

'Aisha passed away in 763 and was buried by the Qarāfah Gate in Cairo, Egypt. (Ebn Jawzi, *Ṣefat aṣ-ṣafwat* ; Sha'rāni, *Ṭabaqāt al-kobrā* , Vol. 1, p. 56.)

'AISHA OF MECCA

'Aisha of Mecca was a devout lady of gnostic character who lived in the latter half of the second century and the early part of the third century, Hegira (circa 800-50) She was a close companion of Abu 'Ali al-Foḍhail Ebn 'Iyāḍh (d. 803)

"When I dwelled in Mecca," Abu 'Abid Qāsem Ebn Salām (d. 838) has recounted, "often I would doze lying on my back with my feet stretched towards the

Ka'ba. One day 'Aisha of Mecca, who was one of the well-known female gnostics of the city, admonished me in this regard."

"Abu 'Abid," she exclaimed, "they say you are a man of knowledge. Listen to a word from me: Never keep anyone's company without *adab* (proper manners), lest your name be scratched from the Register of Proximity. "

This encounter between 'Aisha and Abu 'Abid Ebn Salām, according to Ebn Jawzi (*Şefat aş-şafwat*), occurred during the latter's journey to the Holy City in 834. It seems clear, therefore, that 'Aisha was still living during the years 834 to 838, at the time of Abu 'Abid Ebn Salām's sojourn there. ('Ezzo'd-Din Maḥmud Kāshāni, *Meşbāḥ al-hedāya*, p. 206)

'AISHA OF NISHAPUR

According to the word of Abu 'Abdo'r-Raḥman Moḥammad Solami:

'Aisha of Nishāpur, daughter of Abu 'Othmān, was the most austere and ascetic of all his offspring and surpassed them all in her spiritual state. Her supplications were most often granted. It is reported that 'Aisha once gave her daughter, Omm Aḥmad, the following advice, 'Do not delight in what is merely temporary and disappears. Rejoice rather in the All-Mighty, and take care that you do not fall from His regard. Take care to observe *adab* (proper manners) both outwardly and inwardly. One's inner nature will be punished in accordance with the actions of one's outer being, and whoever acts improperly inwardly, will receive a proportionate inner chastening.'

'Aisha has said, "Lack of acquaintance with the Real (*ḥaqq)* causes disquiet, solitude;" and "disdain towards a servant exhibits lack of knowledge concerning his Master. The lover of the Creator loves the creation as well."

The following saying is also attributed to her, "Do not take joy in people and be not anxious for what has passed away. Rather rejoice in God and be concerned lest you fall from His regard."

'Aisha died in 958. (Ebn Jawzi, *Ṣefat aṣ-ṣafwat*)

'AISHA OF DAMASCUS

This lady of cultivated virtue, the daughter of "Yusof," was one of the renowned gnostics of the tenth century A.H. / fifteenth century A.D.

She was the author of a celebrated commentary on Khwāja 'Abdo'llah Anṣāri's *Pilgrim's Waystations (Manāzel as-sā'erin)* entitled *Concealed Allusions in the Sublime Stations (Al-eshārāt al-khafiya fi'l-manāzel al-auliyā').*

She died in 922 / 1516. (*Rayḥānat al-adab,* Vol. 6, p. 367)

'ATEKAH GHANUYAH

'Atekah was a lady of Bedouin origin, from North Africa. Ḍharār Ṭafāwi relates the following story about her:

I once encountered a devout lady named 'Atekah. She incited me, 'O Ḍharār, by your own Lord, through every way and means, strive to obtain God's favor. When in difficult straits, your problems are solved by His mediation, without either pain or anxiety on your part. Your advantage in this will be plainly evident. Know that those who follow God's commands in this world find no sweeter pleasure in their hearts than increasing their obedience for the sake of proximity to God. In the true seeker's heart, the sweetness of a single hour of obedience to God excels all of the delights and pleasures of the world. Because of God's goodness, the disciple upon God's way never regards what he has given up as a loss. So brother, labor and strive before your time is up and it is too late. Advance yourself in devotional works before it is too late to advance. The world is impure in the mind of one who has comprehended it; unmindful folk distracted by worldly concerns shall soon realize this too.'

At that, she fell silent, rose and left. (Ebn Jawzi, *Ṣefat aṣ-ṣafwat*)

'ABDA, THE SISTER OF SHAIKH DARANI

Abu Solaimān Dārāni (d. 830) relates the following story about his sister 'Abda:

Once, I happened to describe to my sister in particular detail the structure of one of the bridges in Hell. She began to shriek and wail, seemed extremely agitated, and for a night and a day continued like this. Subsequently she quieted down, but whenever I brought the incident to mind, she would begin shrieking all over again. I finally managed one day to ask her what stimulated her shrieks.

'When you described the bridge of Hell,' she replied, 'it appeared to me that my *nafs* was that very bridge. This was sufficient to create that state within me.'

Aḥmad Ebn Abi al-Ḥawāri, a famous disciple of Dārāni) relates that 'Abda once told her brother, "All these poor men are really dead... except for those few whom God has elevated to glory and brought to life through contentment and satisfaction in poverty." (Ebn Jawzi, *Ṣefat aṣ-ṣafwat*)

'OBAYDA, DAUGHTER OF ABI KELAB

'Obayda was a devout lady from Basra of a gnostic temperament. Some have said that she possessed a higher spiritual rank than Rābe'ah. She was a close friend of Mālek Dinār.

'Abda, the daughter of Abi Showāl, has given 'Isā Ebn Marḥum the following account[1] concerning 'Obayda:

> I saw Rābe'ah al-'Adawiya in a dream after she died, and inquired, 'What ever became of 'Obayda, Abi Kalāb's daughter?'
>
> 'O, far beyond me is the station she attained. Never shall I approach her.'

[1] See above, p. 58.

'But how is this, since your spiritual state was higher than hers?'

'Because she did not concern herself with how she passed her nights and days.'

'Obayda is said to have remarked, "Whatever my state is, morning or night, it makes no difference to me."

On the word of Salāma 'Abeda, Sho'aib Ebn Moḥarrez relates that 'Obayda cried for forty years before blindness finally overtook her.

When Salāma Al-Afqam of Ṭafārah asked 'Obayda what she loved most, she replied, "Death."

"Why?" pressed Salāma.

"By God," she avowed, "I fear that as each day dawns I shall perpetuate a sin that shall spell my doom hereafter."

According to 'Abdo'l-'Aziz Ebn Salmān, " 'Obayda and my father associated for twenty years with Mālek Dinar. 'Obayda never bothered Mālek Dinār with any questions, except in one instance when she asked, 'O Mālek, when does the devotee attain a degree beyond all other stations?' Mālek responded, 'When the devotee realizes this station beyond which no other station exists—which you speak of—she loses love and affection for everything, except for attaining union with the utmost haste to God.'

"My father claimed that 'Obaydah wept so much upon hearing this that she swooned and fell.' "

Dā'ud Ebn Moḥabber recorded that Barā' Ghanawi remarked, "Of the contemporaries she left behind on the day she died, no one was as learned as 'Obaydah."

Likewise, 'Abdo'llāh Ebn Rashid Sa'di, who was a close associate of the famous ascetic, 'Abdo'l-Waḥed

Ebn Zayd, recounts, "I encountered many elders, many youths and many female and male devotees of God, yet I never met a woman or man wiser than 'Obayda." (Ebn Jawzi, *Ṣefat aṣ-ṣafwat,* Vol. 4, p.22; Sha'rāni, *Ṭabaqāt al-kobrā*)

AJRADAH 'AMIYAH

Ajradah is to be counted among the pious ladies and mystics of her day. "Her habit," says Rajā, son of Moslem 'Abdi, "was to pray continuously all night and then at sunrise mournfully sing the following lament:

> Till night's end Your worshippers strive towards You, so at the break of dawn, before all, they may be blessed and fortunate through Your mercy. I desire from You nothing else, O God, than that You account me among the company of those who strive forward unto You, that You exalt me to the degree of the righteous near to You and let me join Your charitable servants. Of all who pity, You are the most merciful. Of all who love, You are the most loving, the Greatest of the great, O Generous!

"Falling prostrate on the ground, Ajradah would engage in reading supplications and psalms until sunrise. Such was her habit of devotion for thirty years."

Another Sufi has given the following account:

> Ajradah often visited us, remaining a few days at a time. At night she would stand in the prayer-niche with her clothes and veil on, praying until

dawn. Then she would occupy herself with supplications until sunrise. Either myself or someone else once advised her it would be more propitious to sleep half the night, but Ajradah only wept and admitted that, 'The thought of death doesn't let me sleep.'

Ja'far Ebn Solaimān has related the following description of Ajradah:

> A woman once told my mother that she saw Ajradah on a holiday, covered by a frock, scarf and a darvish mantle all made of wool. As the woman gazed at her, she saw that Ajradah was only skin and bones. Later she was informed that Ajradah had fasted continuously for sixty years. (Ebn Jawzi, *Şefat aş-şafwat*)

AMRAH

Amrah was the wife of Ḥabib 'Ajami (d. 119/737)[1] and a lady of gnostic temperament. According to the statement of Ḥosain Ebn 'Abdo'r-Raḥman:

> Amrah would remain awake the night long and in the morning admonish her husband to rise. 'Day has dawned and night has vanished,' she would say. 'A long path lies before us, our supplies are deficient, and the caravan of workers of good deeds has long since passed us by, leaving us stranded here.' (Ebn Jawzi, *Şefat aş-şafwat*)

[1]See J. Nurbakhsh, *Masters of the Path,* for an account of his life (ed).

'OFAYRA 'ABEDA

Born in Basra, 'Ofayra was a close associate of Mo'ādha 'Adawiya. After she lost her eyesight because of excessive crying, someone asked her whether blindness was difficult to endure. She replied, "More troublesome still is to be veiled from God, the Almighty. It is far more difficult and trying to endure being blind in the heart such that one is unable to discern the purpose of God's will in things." (Jāmi, *Nafaḥāt al-ons*)

Yaḥyā Ebn Basṭām has provided the following account:

> After tears had caused 'Ofayra to go blind, I visited her with one of my friends. Her state moved him to comment to her neighbor, 'How difficult it must be to go blind after once possessing perfect vision!'
>
> Overhearing him, 'Ofayra responded, 'It is far more painful to bear blind-heartedness towards God, than to lack this eyesight that observes the world. I would prefer, by God, that He expropriates every one of my bodily organs and leave me solely with the jewel of His Love.'

Once Ruḥ Ebn Salama Warrāq said to 'Ofayra, "I have heard you never sleep at night." 'Ofayra cried and confessed, "I would prefer to sleep, yet I am unable to. How can I sleep when 'He Whom sleep seizes not, nor slumber' [Koran II: 255] watches over me?"

Deeply affected by her words, Ruḥ Ebn Salama Warrāq writes, "By God I swear, I cried and cried and could only reproach myself saying, 'Alas! Look at my state and witness her state!' "

Mālek Ebn Ḍhaigham states, "Once I heard 'Ofayra say, 'I have sinned against You with all my limbs and disobeyed You as much as possible. I swear by You, that even if You were to assist me in my obedience, I would not be capable of obeying You with all my rebellious limbs.' "

> Sa'id al-'Ami recalls how he suggested to 'Ofayrah that she attempt to lessen her weeping. Bursting out with fresh sobs, she cried, "My son! How can someone who is racked by suffering ever desist from something that may possibly relieve the pain?" Then she began to sob more.

"Once we visited 'Ofayra," Yaḥyā Ebn Rashid recounts, "and one of her nephews had just come back after having been away on a long journey. The glad tidings were delivered to her, but her only reaction was to continue weeping. 'Today is a day for joy, not for tears,' enjoined her relatives. However, her tears just increased in intensity. 'By God,' she cried, 'I swear that in my heart happiness has no home while I remember the Life Hereafter. This event has reminded me how we will all be brought before God. Who can say that he will be happy on that day or full of grief?' Then she fainted." (Ebn Jawzi, *Ṣefat aṣ-ṣafwat*)[1]

[1]In the *Ṭabaqāt al-kobrā* , Vol. I, p. 57, Sha'rāni provides a brief biography of a certain Ḥafira 'Abeda, the contents of which is very similar to the above account of 'Ofayra as 'Ḥafara'. There is also an account of a 'Mo'ira 'Abada by Ebn Jawzi in the *Salwat al-aḥzan* resembling the above biography of 'Ofayra in many details, narration of which we have omitted here.

FAṬEMA BARDA'IYA

This gnostic-minded lady of Ardabil was renowned for a particular genre of paradoxical aphorism that is termed *Shaṭḥ* among the Sufis.[1]

A group of Sufi masters once asked her to provide a commentary on the well-known Prophetic Tradition (*ḥadith*), "I am the Companion of one who remembers Me." She spoke with the questioner for some time and then said, "Remembrance *(dhekr)* is that you contemplate the remembrance of you by Him-who-is-remembered (*madhkur)*, while you never cease to remember Him. Then your remembrance will be annihilated in His remembrance of you, and (only) His remembrance of you will subsist beyond time and space." (Adapted from Jāmi, *Nafaḥāt al-ons*)

FAṬEMA

The Fāṭema referred to here was the sister of the famous Shaikh Abu 'Ali Rudbāri (d 322/934),[2]and the mother of Aḥmad Ebn 'Atā' Rudbāri. She was acclaimed for her ascetic self-denial (*zuhd).*

"One day," Rudbāri relates, "after lecturing on chivalrous generosity (*javānmardi)*, I went to see my sister, who said to me, 'It came to me while meditating that I should urge you towards what will draw you nearer to God. Chivalrous generosity (*javānmardi)* towards mankind consists in treating everyone with

[1] See Ruzbehān Baqli, *Sharḥ-e shaṭḥiyāt* (edited by H. Corbin) Tehran, 1981.

[2]Rudbāri was a master of the Nimatullahi Order. See J. Nurbakhsh, *Masters of the Path.* (ed.).

compassion (*shafaqa),* enduring them with equanimity and perceiving them as above yourself, while witnessing your own faults.' I praised her definition." (Monāwi, *Ṭabaqāt al-auliyā'*)

FAKHR AN-NESA

Aflāki, in the *Menāqeb al-'ārefin* (p. 287), renders the following account of this woman who was known as "The pride of womankind," Fakhr an-Nesā:

> They say that in the era of the great Jalāl ad-Din Rumi, there was a woman saint known as Fakhr an-Nesā. She was a woman of pious and upright character, the Rābe'ah of her age, and performed numerous deeds of charismatic grace (*karāmat*). She was a faithful disciple of Rumi, who would often go to visit her.
>
> Many of Fakhr an-Nesā's companions encouraged her to perform a pilgrimage to the Ka'ba in Mecca. She also sensed a yearning within herself to accomplish the journey. But she informed her comrades, 'First I will consult with Rumi, for it is impossible for me to make a move without his permission and recommendation. I do only as he commands.' So saying, she rose and set out to visit Rumi. She was received by the Master, but before she parted her lips to speak, however, he pronounced, 'It is a good intention you have in mind. May your journey be blessed. I hope we will be in each other's company.' Then he bowed his head, immersing himself in silence. Rumi's statement left his disciples dumbfounded, wondering about the true

nature of their telepathic communication.

That night, she remained in Rumi's house. Shortly after midnight, the master climbed onto the roof to engage in his nightly devotions. When he completed his prayers, he began to shout loudly and excitedly. Then he signaled with his hand through the skylight in the roof for Fakhr an-Nesā to come up.

Once upon the roof, Rumi ordered her, 'Look up. The Goal has presented itself to you.' Doing so, she beheld the Ka'ba, revolving and circumambulating in the sky above Rumi's head. The sight to her was clearly visible without doubt, or trace of ambiguity. Fakhr an-Nesā gasped and was overcome by awe and bewilderment. Regaining her senses she submitted herself totally to God and utterly abandoned her wish to go to Mecca.

FAṬEMA BENT AL-MOTHANNA

Ebn 'Arabi, in his *Meccan Revelations (Fotuḥāt al-makkiyah)*, gives the following account of Fāṭema Bent al-Mothanna:

> I waited on her with all my soul for many years; at that time she was ninety-five years of age. The delicacy and freshness of her visage, however, made me ashamed to look at her. Most people who saw her thought she was fourteen years old. She possessed a wondrously elevated state with God and preferred my company over that of all the contemporaries of her day who waited upon her. She said of me, 'I have never seen the likes of that fellow. He comes to visit

me with his total being, and when he departs, he goes away with his whole being, no residue of himself is left behind with me.'

Ebn 'Arabi also relates that he once heard her remark, "I am surprised when people who claim to love God, the Exalted, still do not rejoice in Him, since by means of Him they behold everything and even for a blink of an eye His omniscient attention and regard is not withdrawn from them. How can these men profess love of God, and still weep?"

On another occasion, Ebn 'Arabi recounts:

> We were sitting before Fāṭema when a poor lady visitor came in complaining to us that her husband had gone to a distant city intending to betroth a second wife. I asked her if she desired that he return and she answered in the affirmative. Turning to Fāṭema I said, 'Do you hear what she says?' She asked me what it was I had in mind I said, 'True fulfillment of her need would be for her husband to return.' Fāṭemah responded, 'I heard and will obey. I shall send off the *Fāteḥat al-ketāb*[1] this very instant and command it to fetch her husband.'
>
> She then began to recite the *Fāteḥah,* while I accompanied her. As we read the *Fāteḥah,* a corporeal form came into being which she sent off, saying 'O *Fāteḥat al-ketāb,* go to such-and-such a city, where you will find this woman's husband. Do not part from him until you bring him back here.'

[1] The opening chapter of the Koran, also called *Ṣurat al-Ḥamd,* the chapter of Praise (ed.).

The amount of time that elapsed between sending off the *Fāteḥah* and her husband's return was no more than it would have taken to normally traverse that distance. (Jāmi, *Nafaḥāt al-ons*)

In another of his books, Ebn 'Arabi gives the following description of Fāṭema:

> She lived at Seville. When I met her she was in her nineties and only ate the scraps left by people at their doors. Although she was so old and ate so little, I was almost ashamed to look at her face when I sat with her, it was so rosy and soft.
>
> Although God offered to her His Kingdom, she refused, saying, 'You are all, all else is inauspicious for me.' Her devotion to God was profound. Looking at her in a purely superficial way one might have thought she was a simpleton, to which she would have replied that he who knows not his Lord is the real simpleton. She was indeed a mercy to the world.
>
> Once, on the night of the Festival, Abū 'Amir, the muezzin, struck her with his whip in the mosque. She gave him a look and left the place feeling very angry with him. In the morning she heard him calling to prayer and said, 'O my Lord, do not rebuke me that I was affected by one who calls Your Name in the darkness of the night while other men sleep, for it is my Beloved who is mentioned on his lips. O God, do not censure him because of my feeling against him.'
>
> The next morning the jurists of the locality went, after the Festival prayer, to convey their respects to the Sultan. This muezzin, full of

worldly aspiration, went in with them. When the Sultan enquired who the fellow might be, he was told that it was only the muezzin. Then the Sultan asked who had allowed him to come in with the jurists and ordered him to be thrown out, which he was. However, after someone had pleaded with the Sultan on his behalf, and he was let off, although the Sultan had intended to punish him. Fāṭema heard about this incident and said, 'I know about it, and if I had not prayed for leniency for him he would have been executed.' Her spiritual influence was very great indeed. After this she died. (Ebn 'Arabi, *Resāla ruḥ al-qods*)[1]

FAṬEMA OF EGYPT

This Fāṭema was the daughter of 'Abdo'r-Raḥmān al-Ghaffār Ḥarrāni. Originally from Baghdad, she later moved to Egypt. She was known as Omm Moḥammad. In Egypt she transmitted traditions and lived to over eighty years of age. Because she wore only woolen attire and for sixty years slept without bedding on her prayer-mat, she is accounted as a Sufi. In 924 she passed away. (Ebn Jawzi, *Ṣefat aṣ-ṣafwat*)

FAṬEMA

She was the daughter of Moḥammad Ebn Monkader. Ebrāhim Moslem Qorashi renders the following account of her:

Every day Fāṭema fasted. At nightfall with a

[1] Translated by R.W.J. Austin, *Sufis of Andalusa*, pp. 143-44.

sorrowful voice she would lament, 'Night has now covered all with darkness. Every friend has secluded himself with his friend, yet I have chosen You alone to retire with, O Beloved, that You may free me from the Fire.' (Ebn Jawzi, *Şefat aş-şafwat*)

FAṬEMA OF BAGHDAD

Fāṭema, also known as Omm Zaynab, was the daughter of 'Abbās. She was proficient as a judge, jurisprudent, teacher, scholar, devotee, ascetic and Sufi. She came from the outskirts of Baghdad and followed Imam Ḥanbal in jurisprudence. Besides presiding over a small circle of women whom she instructed, she would often go up on the pulpit to deliver sermons to the public. Ebn Taymiyah relates, "It unsettled my lower soul (*nafs)* that she went up on the pulpit to deliver public sermons, and I wished to forbid her, till one night I beheld the Prophet Moḥammad in a dream and he rebuked me, saying 'This lady performs good works.' "

Fāṭema passed away in 1314 in Cairo. (Shaikh Yusef Nabahāni, *Jame' al-karāmat al-auliyā')* as recounted by Monawi)

FAṬEMA OF NISHAPUR

She is to accounted among the great gnostics and Sufis of her age. She lived in Khorasan, and Bāyazid Bastāmi often sought out her company, extolling her highly. She sometimes resided in Mecca, often journeying from there to Jerusalem and back.

Dho'n-Nun Mesri, it is said, was her acquaintance. On one occasion she sent him a gift. He refused to accept it, objecting that it was a sign of imperfection and inadequacy to accept anything from women. Fāṭema replied, "Nothing is more virtuous or greater for a Sufi in this world than to lift his view beyond the (temporal) causes (behind phenomena)."

Bāyazid Bastāmi has said, "In my life I only encountered one *real* man and one *real* woman — Fāṭema of Nishāpur. There was no station (on the way) about which I told her that she had not already undergone."

A master once asked Dho'n-Nun Meṣri, "Who, in your opinion, is the highest among the Sufis?"

"A lady in Mecca, called Fāṭemah Nishāpuri, whose discourse displayed a profound apprehension of the inner meanings of the Koran which were astounding," replied Dho'n-Nun. Further pressed to comment on Fāṭema, he added, "She is of the saints of God, and my teacher."

Once in Jerusalem, Dho'n-Nun requested that Fāṭema give him some words of counsel. She exhorted him, "In all your actions, watch that you act with sincerity and in opposition to your lower soul (*nafs*)."

Fāṭema of Nishāpur's maxims include:

> Whoever doesn't have God in his consciousness, is erring and in delusion, whatever language he speaks, whatever company he keeps. Yet, whoever holds God's company never speaks except with sincerity and assiduously adheres to a humble reserve and earnest devotion in his conduct.

In this day and age, a man of true spiritual honesty and piety is buffeted by an ocean whose waves distress him. His entreaty to God is to liberate him, to grant him salvation from its waves.

One who works for the vision of the Truth is a gnostic (*'āref*)and whoever's conduct is based on the fact that God is constantly observing him, is a devotee.

Fāṭema died while performing the lesser pilgrimage in 838. (Jāmi, *Nafaḥāt al-ons;* Ebn Jawzi, *Ṣefat aṣ-ṣafwat;* Sha'rāni, *Ṭabaqāt al-kobrā)*

FEḌHA

Shaikh Abo'r-Rabi' Mālaqi narrates what is known of Feḍha in the following account:

> After hearing of a holy woman who lived in a rural area, I went out to pay my respects to her in order to gather more knowledge concerning certain miracles for which she was widely acclaimed. She was known as Feḍha. On arriving at her village I was notified that she owned a sheep out of which flowed flavored milk. I bought a cup and then went to her house to greet her.
>
> When I met her, I told her I wished to witness what people had said concerning her sheep. She presented the sheep to me and milked it into my cup. When I drank the contents, it was indeed milk and honey, so I asked her to recount the tale

of this miracle.

'Once we had a sheep,' she confessed, 'which my husband, a man of good character, intended to sacrifice on a certain religious holiday. However, we were quite poor and I objected, saying it was quite within the bounds of the canon law to forego its sacrifice, for God had to be aware of our need for it. It so happened that a guest came to stay with us that day, and noting the necessity of acting graciously to all guests, I advised my husband to kill the sheep. I added, however, that he should do so out of the sight of our children, since seeing the animal slaughtered would make them cry.

'My husband took the sheep behind the back wall to sacrifice. Then all at once, I saw a sheep jump over the wall into the yard. I thought that the sheep perhaps had fled from my husband. But when I went behind the back wall, I saw him just removing the sheep's skin.

'Utterly dumbfounded, I told my husband what I had seen. 'Perhaps the Almighty,' he philosophized, 'has given us another sheep better than the one we sacrificed for the guest.'

At this point, Feḍha concluded her story by remarking, 'O son, this sheep grazes in the hearts of disciples. If their hearts are joyous, its milk likewise is sweet, but if their hearts are offended, its milk likewise is sour. So endeavor to delight their hearts.'

Commenting on Feḍha's statement, Imam Yāfe'i has said, "By disciples, Feḍha was actually referring to her husband. However, she spoke generally of disciples in order to conceal and disguise as well as to encourage real disciples to be happy at heart. What

4

Drawing of a woman milking her cow. Persian Esphahan seventeenth century. B.M. 1074-6-17-03 (f. 99) she really meant was that joy of heart should be happiness based on what we inwardly sense; therefore one should always strive to rejoice within one's heart, till everyone around you also rejoices." (Jāmi, *Nafaḥāt, al-ons*)

FAKHRIYA

Fakhriya was the daughter of 'Othmān, known as 'Yusef'. A native of Basra, Iraq, she engaged in periodic fasts and was steadfast in maintaining a nightly vigil of prayer. She was the greatest Sufi of her time, totally unique among all the other women of her day.

Once, for forty days, she remained standing by the door of the Jerusalem mosque, constantly performing her prayers while waiting for its gates to open. She was always the first person to enter and last to leave the mosque. Her grace (*karāmāt*) was extraordinary.

Fakhriya always wished to die in Mecca and be buried next to Khadija, Mother of the Believers.[1] God granted her prayer, and she was subsequently entombed there after her death in 1352. (Nabahāni, *Jame' Karāmat al-auliyā'*)

KORDIYA ḤAFṢA

Kordiya came from Basra (or Ahwaz, according to Jāmi) and was the daughter of 'Omar. She was companion of Sha'wāna, whose biography was given above.

[1]Moḥammad's first wife (ed.).

One night she was with Sha'wāna and nodded off to sleep. Sha'wānah kicked her and said, "Arise! This is no place to doze off, Kordiya—sleep belongs to the tomb."

When asked how she had benefitted from Sha'wāna's company, she replied, "From the very first day that I began to wait on her, I lost all interest in the world, and all anxiety from where my next meal was to come from deserted me. I neither accounted any Muslim as insignificant, nor considered any worldly person as elevated. (Jami, *Nafaḥāt al-ons* ; Ebn Jawzi, *Ṣefat aṣ-ṣafwat*)

LOBABAH MOTA'ABEDAH

A resident of Jerusalem, Lobābah is renowned for having declared, "Before God, I am ashamed that He sees me engaged in ought besides Him."

Once someone voiced their intention of performing the pilgrimage to Mecca and asked Lobāba what he should pray for. She responded, "Supplicate to His Highness that He be content with you, and entreat Him to lift you up to attain the station of those who rejoice and are contented with Him, and beg Him to bring you into the company of His saints."

Concerning her spiritual life, Lobāba has said:

> I exerted myself in worship (of God) until I reached tranquillity. When I wearied of seeing people, God gave me intimacy in His remembrance (*dhekr)*. When people tired me, I would be given ease by finding time for my devotions, and accomplishing His service. (Jāmi, *Nafaḥāt al-ons* ; Ebn Jawzi, *Ṣefat aṣ-ṣafwat*)

The father of Māmā 'Eṣmat was a certain Bābā Faqih Aḥmad Asbosti who originally came from Konya, Turkey. He was a well-known jurisprudent who was said to belong to the Ahari Sufi Order. He subsequently moved to Asbost, a village outside of Tabriz, between Sardrud and Asku, near the village of Esfahlān.

Karbālā'i in the *Rawḍhāt al-jenān*, provides the following account of Aḥmad Asbosti's daughter, Māmā 'Eṣmat:

> Māmā 'Eṣmat was the queen of the gnostic women of her time, highly acclaimed and deeply venerated for her saintliness among the company of the righteous. She had attained to remarkably exalted spiritual stations and experienced wondrous mystical states. Her transcendental doctrine was infused with Divine Almightiness and Majesty. It is related that once, while strolling in her garden, she happened to pass by a pear tree of wide girth. Her headscarf became ensnared in the tree's branches, and was torn from her head. By strength of her spiritual will alone, she tore the tree from its roots and cast it down. When she returned to her normal state, people begged her to tell them by what state she had been possessed. She replied, 'It came from elsewhere than I know or comprehend. I am impotent in myself to pluck out even a piece of straw from an adobe wall.'

It is related from reliable sources that Māmā 'Eṣmat had a gardener who engaged in farming for her. On one occasion when occupied in planting her land, Māmā criticized his method of sowing the seed. The unfortunate man was unable to tolerate her rebuke, and replied rudely, "Woman, what do you know of farming and the business of planting? Mind your own business!"

Stirred by the overwhelming power of God's Almightiness (*jalāliyat)* Māmā explained, "The evil hour of your death has arrived, and you don't approve of me?" At that same moment, the gardener keeled over and died at her feet.

After he was carried away and buried, Māmā came to his cottage to offer her condolences, as was the local custom. She composed a brief eulogy, a stanza of two couplets in the local dialect, which was recited at his funeral.

Another tale of Māmā 'Eṣmat relates to a Sufi master who was connected to her through spiritual companionship, a certain Kamal ad-Din Baku'i, involving his sojourn to Mecca accompanied by the chief Shaikh of Tabriz.

> While travelling through the great wilderness of Arabia, both men were suddenly overwhelmed by great thirst, no water being available anywhere. Suddenly, the pair spotted a female figure emerging from the desert waste, draped in a veil. She carried a particular red pitcher, of Tabrizi make, full of ice, in her hand, and coming forward, presented the pitcher to Kamal ad-Din. He availed himself of the water, confirming with presence of heart and full sober consciousness of the physical fact of his drinking, passing the pitcher on to the Shaikh and the rest of the

company travelling with him. When all had quenched their thirst , the lady took the pitcher and vanished from sight. The Shaikh turned to Kamal Ad-Din and asked him, 'Who is that gnostic lady saint, (*waliya-ye 'aref)* through whose succour our thirsty party was rescued from this dreadful desert?' Kamal ad-Din maintained his peace and refused to reveal the identity of the lady, only commenting, 'Later it will be clear to you.' After completing their pilgrimage to Mecca, the company returned to Tabriz. Not long after their return, Kamal ad-Din decided to pay Māmā 'Eṣmat a visit. Accompanied by the Shaikh of Tabriz and a few other friends, they set out for the village of Asbost. Reaching the house of Māmā 'Eṣmat, they were entertained by their hostess. The Shaikh of Tabriz's eye fell on a certain pitcher, the same kind, or an identical replica of which had fostered their rescue in the desert on the way to Mecca. At once he remembered their journey, the mysterious apparition of the veiled woman carrying a pitcher full of ice. Kamal Ad-Din leaned over to him and put his finger to his lip, saying, in a whisper, 'The secrets of God's Friends should always be concealed and secreted, never revealed to the public eye.'

A wellknown man from the nearby village of Esfahlan recounted the following story concerning Māmā 'Eṣmat.

There was once a wedding ceremony in Asbost, and my mother went there. At that time, I was a young boy, so young in fact, that the women did not feel it necessary to veil themselves from me, as they did from older men. After the wedding ceremony, my mother spent the night in the house of Māmā 'Eşmat. All the ladies curled up in their respective corners in their bedrolls to sleep, and the lights of the house were extinguished. One particular lady, however, who was usually in the service of Māmā 'Eşmat, spent the night awake, occupied with her semi-audible commemoration of God *(dhekr).* Suddenly Māmā 'Eşmat was overcome by an ecstatic state. All the women awoke in the house, and sat in their corners, watching. I crawled over by my mother's side and contemplated the scene. It seemed as if the attire of Māmā 'Eşmat was full of light, the radiance of the rays of which were shown forth in variegated colors quite visibly to the entire gathering, illuminating the house, as if many candles therein had been lit. It is related that most of the time when Māmā 'Eşmat was overcome with raptures and ecstasies, bright lights could be witnessed shining from her sleeves and her skirt, and the following couplet by her bears witness to this idea:

I entered into this poverty as a poor beggar,
without capital,
All pearls and jewels I sell from the market of
Nothingness.

The princes and nobility of her day and age had total faith and complete devotion to her, insofar as she exemplified a pattern of spiritual behavior appealing to all classes of people, both nobles and commoners alike. It is recounted that one day the mother of his Imperial Majesty Jahānshāh (d. 1467), Shekkar Khatun, paid

Māmā 'Eṣmat a visit. During her stay in the house of the saint, it so happened that Jahānshāh was but a child. As he crawled about the room, he came close to the feet of the saint. She looked down and exclaimed, 'This boy of yours shall one day be a great king,' and in the end her prediction proved true.

Māmā Eṣmat's miracle working abilities and feats shattering the laws of nature, which made her so renowned in her lifetime, were likewise apparent after her demise. It is related that in 1535 Ḥāji Qāsem Separdus, a Sufi of an ardorous disposition, and one of the sons of the master Ḥaji Ḥassan Zatāb, (who in turn also related to the other Sufi teachers of the village of Asbost), was transported from himself by the rapture of Divine attraction. His disposition was so violent that he was taken to the neighboring village of Asbost and incarcerated in one of the houses which used to belong to Māmā 'Eṣmat. They were forced to restrain him and tie down his hands. One of the sons of the Sufi master of Asbost, by the name of Sayedi Khwājegi, assumed the responsibility of taking care of him, and in the words of that person, 'The attraction experienced and the rapture felt by Qāsem Sefardus was so intense that no person was safe to be left with him, since it was quite possible that he would injure someone. Since his hands were totally restrained and tightly bound they began to swell, and the inflammation was such that his hands were rendered incapable of use. For instance, when we would place a turban on his head and wind it around his brow, he would violently toss his head back and throw it off.' After a time, Qāsem cried out, amid his wailing, mentioning my name. I went immediately to the house, and I saw him sitting on his two knees kneeling and the turban wound neatly about his head. I was very surprised. His hands had been so inflamed that they were incapable by themselves of winding a turban.

I Asked after his health, and he replyed,

'At this very moment, Māmā 'Eṣmat appeared to me and consoled me and wound this turban about my head, and then, humming a certain spiritual tune silently to herself, departed.'

After this experience he recovered his senses, his lunacy and wildness totally vanishing.

Māmā 'Eṣmat died a natural death of physical causes. When she departed from this world, she was taken to the mortuary where she was washed by the mortician, who in the process of scrubbing down her body noticed on her finger a golden ring which Māmā 'Eṣmat had placed there as wages to be given to the mortician. Now the mortician was in quite a haste, and was very rude in her efforts to remove the ring. Pulling the ring off, Māmā 'Eṣmat raised her hand and slapped the mortician across the face.

At the time of the death of Māmā 'Eṣmat, Kamāl ad-Din Baku'i was still living. He spent three nights at the gravesite, as she had bidden him to do before she died. The death of Kamal ad-Din Baku'i occurred during the reign of Sultan Qarā-Yusef (d. 1433). Reverend Māmā was one of the elect among the company of the righteous, who had attained remarkably elevated stations and was dominated by an exalted sense of Divine majesty. She was often overcome by marvelous states and rapture which made her widely acclaimed.

MARYAM OF BASRA

She was one of the companions of Rābe'ah who attended on the latter's needs, surviving Rābe'ah by a few years. Her discourses on love were well-known, and when the subject of love was raised, she would often faint. Her death occurred during a certain spiritual assembly wherein the preacher spoke on the matter of love; Maryam was deeply affected, had a heart attack, and died.

When alive, Maryam claimed that attaining a means for a livelihood never raised a problem for her.[1] Once she heard this verse, "In heaven is your sustenance and that which you are promised" [Koran LI:22] Maryam ceased to feel it necessary to labor to make a living. At dusk, Maryam would rise to her feet, recounts Ebn Jawzi, and begin to pray, taking the verse "God is gracious to his servants" [Koran XLII:19] as her litany until the break of dawn. (Jāmi, *Nafaḥāt al-ons* ; Ebn Jawzi, *Ṣefat aṣ-ṣafwat*)

MESKINA ṬEFLAWIYA

Meskina was an inhabitant of Basra. According to Esḥāq Ebn Ebrāhim, 'Ammār Rāheb has provided the following account of a dream involving Meskina:

[1] Since Sufis believe that God is the Provider.

She was one of those who attended the Sufi assemblies of remembrance (*dhekr*). When I saw her (in a dream), I said, 'Well done, well done, O Meskina!'

She merely responded, 'Nevermore, nevermore, O Ammār. Meskina[1] has departed, and Great Wealth has arrived.'

'What has happened to you?' I questioned.

'How can you ask such a question,' she rebuked me, 'of someone who experiences herself surrounded by paradise on every side, and may pass freely wherever she wishes therein?'

I then said, 'May God have mercy on You! How did this grace come to you?'

She responded, 'By presence in assemblies of remembrance and maintaining constancy before God.' (Ebn Jawzi, *Ṣefat aṣ-ṣafwat*)

MO'ADHA 'ADAWIYA

Mo'ādha, who lived in the era of Rābe'ah 'Adawiya and benefited from her company, was the daughter of 'Abdo'llāh 'Adawiya and was surnamed Omm Ṣahbā.

When Mo'ādha was reproached for overworking herself, she replied, "There is no harm in what I'm doing. On the contrary, I have only put off sleeping at night until daytime and stopped eating during the day to take my meals at night."

According to some accounts, as each day arrived Mo'ādha would say, "Since today I shall die, I won't sleep till night-time." But when night came, she would

[1] The literal meaning of the word *meskina* is destitute.

say, "This night I shall die, so I won't sleep until morning." In the cold season she would dress herself in thin garments so the cold would hinder her from drowsing.

A lady who waited on Mo'ādha recounted that she always used to maintain a night vigil, praying until dawn. Whenever sleep overcame her, she would pace the courtyard of her house, and censure herself, "O lower soul (*nafs)*, sleep lies before you, and if you die now, you shall slumber even longer in the tomb, and the sleep of death shall either be filled with delight, or marred by bitter regret and compunction." She would recite this sentence until the break of day.

According to Asiya, the daughter of 'Omar 'Adawiya, Mo'ādha was accustomed to performing six hundred prostrations of prayer in every twenty-four hours. Part of the night she kept awake reading the Koran. It is said that she once remarked, "I wonder at 0the eye that dozes, knowing the long dark slumber of the grave before it."

A certain Abu Sawār 'Adawiya has said of her, "The tribe of Bani 'Adi in this town excels everyone else in spiritual combat (*mojāheda).* Among them Abu Saḥbā never sleeps, nor does he eat during the day, while his wife, Mo'ādha, has not raised her head to look at the skies for the last forty years."

One of the women of the tribe of Bani 'Adi who Mo'ādhi nursed as an infant, related that the saintly lady once advised her, "My girl, fear God, yet have hope in Him. I have witnessed how those who place their hopes in God are received with honors and raised to high ranks in the Divine Presence, while those who fear Him long for security upon that day." Then she broke down in tears and fainted.

Ḥamād Ebn Salmat recounted how Thābet Banāni informed him that when Abu Saḥbā turned to his son, and urged, "Go, son, and fight, so that I can bring you to reckoning on the Way of God," his son stepped forward, fighting until death. Subsequently his father also advanced and met death.

Women gathered around Mo'ādha to offer their condolences. She responded, "Welcome ladies, if you have come here to offer your congratulations to me, but if you have come with anything else in mind, please go home."

After her husband and son were slain, Salmeh Ebn Ḥasān 'Adawiya related, Mo'ādha refused to remarry and died a widow. Another woman who Mo'ādha nursed as an infant, by the name of Omm Sawād, the daughter of Zayd 'Adawiya, records this remark of Mo'ādha:

> Since the day that Abu Ṣahbā and his son were martyred, I swear by God that I feel no interest in remaining in the world, neither tasting the delights of life, nor breathing in its pleasant breezes attract me. Yet insofar as existence afford me a means to worship and so to approach God, I live and love life, hoping to be reunited with my husband and son in heaven.

According to accounts of Ruḥ Ebn Salmah Warrāq and 'Ofayra 'Abeda, while Mo'ādha was on her deathbed, she suddenly cried out, then began to laugh. When asked for an explanation, she replied, "My crying out was from fear of being deprived in the future of fasting, prayer and recollection of God. But my laughter was because I saw Abu Ṣahbā in a vision, enter into a house attired in green, along with a great number of people whose like I had not seen in this world. So I laughed for his sake, for after this [experience], I saw there were no further religious obligations for me to fulfill." Saying this, she died, shortly before the appointed time for ritual prayers.

It is further recounted that Mo'ādha knew 'A'eshah (the Prophet's wife), and related traditions concerning the Prophet directly from her. In turn, Ḥasan al-Baṣri, Abu Qallāba and Yazid al-Rashk are said to have related traditions from Mo'ādha. (Ebn Jawzi, *Ṣefat aṣ-ṣafwat;* Sha'rani, *Ṭabāqāt al-kobrā,* Vol. I, p. 56; Jāmi, *Nafaḥāt al-ons*)

MAYMUNA SIYAH

The following account of Maymuna has been given by 'Abdo'l Wāḥed Ebn Zayd to Foḍail Ebn 'Iyāz:[1]

> For three consecutive nights I begged God to make manifest to me who was to be my companion in Paradise. On the third night, I dreamt that someone said, 'O Servant of God, your friend in Heaven shall be Maymuna Siyāh.' Asking where she was to be found, I was told that she belonged to such-and-such a family in Kufa.

[1] A great Sufi master who died in 803 . See 'Aṭṭār, *Memoirs of the Saints,* p. 52. (ed.)

The following day I journeyed to Kufa and sought out this woman. I was told by the townspeople that she was a madwoman who worked as a shepherdess. Informing them of my desire to meet her, I was directed to go into the desert. Out in the desert I found her praying. She had placed a staff before her and was dressed in a woolen cloak upon which was inscribed, 'I will never buy nor sell.' Her flock of sheep were pastured together with wolves. The wolves didn't attack the sheep, nor did the sheep fear the wolves. When she realized I was there, she exclaimed, 'Return, Ebn Zayd, the time predestined has not yet arrived.'

God bless you! I exclaimed. Who told you I am Ebn Zayd?

'Are you not aware,' she replied, 'of the Prophetic Tradition (*ḥadith*) which tells us "The spirits are like armies arranged in ranks. Those who have recognized one another in this world will become friends, and those who have not recognized one another will be in conflict?" '

When I asked her to advise me, she replied, 'I am surprised that a preacher wants someone else to preach to him!' Then she added, 'O Ebn Zayd, I have heard that any slave of God who gives something of the world away in charity is granted something similar in return. But someone from whom the love of solitude with God is taken away receives distance after proximity and fearful loneliness after intimacy.'

I begged her to tell me her secret and explain how her sheep could be pastured with wolves. In response, she said, 'Since I have arranged my affairs between myself and God, He likewise has established peace between the wolves and the sheep.'[1]

In another account, Rabi' Ebn Khitham is said to have been told in a dream that Maymuna was to be his future wife in heaven. On awakening, he sought her out and found her herding sheep. He has described his meeting with her as follows:

> I reflected that I would wait and observe her doings. I saw her continually occupied in ritual prayers. At nightfall I went to her house. She obtained milk for us, drank some, and then gave some to me. On the third day I said to her, 'Why do you never drink any other milk besides that of this female sheep?' She didn't immediately respond, but I persisted in my question.
>
> 'Because this sheep,' she finally replied, 'has been given to me, I drink its milk and give it to whomever I like.'
>
> 'And you have no other work besides this?' I asked.
>
> 'No,' replied Maymuna, 'Neither morning nor evening do I want anything but God. I am thoroughly content with what has been allotted to me.'
>
> Expecting to surprise and shock her, I then said to Maymuna, 'Do you know that you are to be my wife in Heaven?'
>
> 'Are you then Rabi' Ebn Khitham?' she responded.
>
> 'Yes,' I confessed, realizing that she already knew. (Nabahāni, *Jame' karāmat al-auliyā'*)

---

[1] In the *Ketāb al-'oqalā' al-majā'nim* Maymuna's reply is cited as follows: Since all ceremony has been lifted between myself and the One before Whom I stand, all fear between the wolves and the sheep, too, is gone.

MALIKA, DAUGHTER OF MONKADER

Malika was a pious lady from Medina. Musā Ebn 'Abdo'l Mālek Abu 'Abdo'r-Raḥman Marwazi retells the following account of Mālek Dinār[1] concerning Malika:

> In the midst of circumambulating the Ka'ba, I beheld a woman standing beside the Black Stone, crying out in a shrill voice, 'The distance is far from which I have come, hopeful of Your generosity. Enable me to attain Your bounty till I become heedless of all other goodness, You who are famed for Your Goodness!'
>
> A short while later, I made the acquaintance of Ayyub Sakhtiyāni and together we set out to visit Malika in her home. Ayyub greeted her first and asked her to favor him with some advice. She replied, 'My heart will have no complaints of God. A number of people are opposed to me, however, and seek to prevent me from my devotions to God, even though I am only preoccupied in attempting to rectify my own book of deeds.'
>
> Though Ayyub professed that he had never before spoken to the lady, he suggested, 'Perhaps to marry a gentleman might assist you in your endeavors.'
>
> Malika replied, 'If it were to be either Mālek Dinār or Ayyub Sakhtiyāni, it would not be to my liking."
>
> 'I am Mālek Dinār and this fellow here is Ayyub Sakhtiyāni,' I then confessed.

---

[1] A famous scholar of traditions, disciple of Ḥasan of Basra, and acquaintance of Rābe'ah Adawiyya, who died in 130 / 748.

'Too bad!' remarked Malika, 'I imagined you two to be so absorbed in remembrance of God as to have no time for women. I had supposed you would prefer prayer.'

When we asked her name, we were told she was called Malika, the daughter of Monkader.

In a similar account Abu Khāled Barrād writes that he once suggested to Malika that she reduce the amount of some of her devotionssome of her devotions. She responded by saying, "Leave me be. I am engaged with my book of deeds." (Ebn Jawzi, *Şefat aş-şafwat*)

MANQUSA, DAUGHTER OF ZAYD EBN ABOL-FAWARES

It is said that upon the death of her son, Manqusa laid her brow on his tombstone and prayed as follows:

> By God, it is better, O son, that I sent you along ahead of me, rather than after me. Waiting patiently for you is better than worrying about you. Though being away from you grieves me, expecting God to reward you is to be preferred. (Sha'rani, *Tabaqāt al-kobra*)

MO'MENA, DAUGHTER OF BOHLUL

'Isā Ebn Esḥāq Anṣāri cites the following saying of Mo'menah, "There is no bounty besides intimacy with God and concordance with His will." (Ebn Jawzi, *Şefat aş-şafwat*)

MAYMUNA, SISTER OF EBRAHIM EBN AḤMAD KHAWAṢṢ[1]

Maymuna was reputed to be her brother's equal in asceticism, piety and reliance on God. Aḥmad Ebn Sālem recounts the story of a man who went to see Ebrāhim Khawaṣṣ. When he knocked on the door, he was met by Maymanu, Ebrāhim's sister, who asked his name and what he wanted. He introduced himself and asked for Ebrāhim Khawaṣṣ.

"He has gone out," she told him.

"When will he return?"

Maymuna replied, "How can someone who has surrendered his life to another know when he is returning?" (Ebn Jawzi, *Ṣefat aṣ-ṣafwat*)

LADY NANA

Lady Nana was born into a noble family, and was a woman of great sensitivity and spiritual awareness. Shaikh Ali Khosrowshāhi recounted that once Amir Badro'd,Din Lālah (1436-1501) decided to visit some of the tombs of the local Tabrizi masters. He brought an embroidered cloth with him, and gave it to me, requesting me to deliver it to Nana, saying, "Tell her that I pray for her soul, and entreat her to recite the Fāteha on my behalf." I did as he asked, delivering the present to Nana and asking her to supplicate on his behalf. Nana prayed and wept, saying, "Who am I that they should wish me to pray for them? In this gesture they demonstrate merely their own magnanimity."

[1] A famous ascetic and Sufi who was a companion of Al-Jonayd. He died in 904 (ed.).

It has also been related that Nana could hold eggs in her hands and cook them over a fire, but her hands were never burnt. (Ebn Karbalāi, *Rauḍhāt al-Jenān*)

NAQISH, DAUGHTER OF SALEM

Abu Mowerreq recounts that someone once heard Naqish make the following supplication in Mecca:

> O Master of slaves, I am faced with tribulation. At this station, people take refuge in Your mercy from Your anger, and in Your compassion from Your wrath. O Companion of the repentant! O Pure Bounty, Lord of all Grace and Generosity! Increase the causes of my trust in you. Concentrate the motives of my love for You. Brighten my eyes in adoration of You.

Elsewhere, relates Abu Mowerreq, Naqish was heard to make the following prayer:

> O Lord of all slaves! My work is in dire straits. I have painted my eyelids with the collyrium of Love's grief. By Your Glory, I swear I never shall laugh until I fathom where my ultimate abode and place of rest shall be.

Beholding the populace with their hands raised in supplication, she would pray:

> O Creator, You have caused the people to attain to this station through fears of the inferno—O You, Who are my eye's light and Light of the eyes of every good person who prays, yearns and

hopes for Your grace.

When the people departed, however, she would lay her face on the earth and weep and lament, "My heart still does not despair, though men have turned away from You." (Ebn Jawzi, *Ṣefat aṣ-ṣafwat*)

NAFISA

Nafisa was the daughter of Moḥammad Ḥasan, who was the son of 'Ali Zayno'l-'Abidin[1], and thus a direct decendent of the Prophet. She was born in Mecca and subsequently migrated with her husband, Eshāq, son of Ja'far Sādeq (702-765), to Egypt, where she resided for seven years. Some historians maintain that she was accompanied by her father, Ḥasan, whose grave is in Egypt, but this is doubtful.

Nafisa was a devout woman, renowned for her abstinence. The Egyptians had a great admiration for her, and it is said that when Imam Shāfe'i went to Egypt, he heard her relate Prophetic Traditions, which he subsequently transmitted on her word alone.

When Imam Shāfe'i passed away, Nafisa said the prayers for the dead over his corpse in her own house. She then took up residence at the site of his grave until she died in 823.(Sha'rāni, *Tabaqāt al-kobrā,* Vol. I, p. 58; Ebn Khallekān, *Wafayāt al-a'yan)*

A Sufi master of Nafisa's time recounts that in her day there was an unjust ruler who wished to torture a certain person. The victim sought refuge with Nafisa. She prayed for him and then told him he might leave, instructing him, "God Almighty will veil the eyes of the

[1] The fourth Shi'ite Imam (658-713).

unjust from perceiving who you are."

The man went among the prince's companions and stood before his tormentor. "Where is so-and-so?" the prince inquired of his companions. They told him, "He is standing here right in front of you." The prince replied, "But, by God, I don't see him." His companions answered, "The man has visited Nafisa and requested that she pray for him. After praying she informed him that God had concealed him from the sight of the unjust." Abashed, the prince confessed, "So, my oppression has reached such extremes that merely through people's prayer's, God veils my eyes from beholding the oppressed! O Lord! I repent! To You I return."

When the prince raised his head, he saw the man standing before him. He prayed for him, kissed his head, and gave him a rich set of clothes to wear. Then he sent the man on his way in gratitude. Afterwards, the prince gathered all his wealth together and gave it away to the poor, sending one hundred thousand dirhams to Lady Nafisa as a thanksgiving offering that a servant of God had returned to Him. Nafisah took and money and distributed it amongst the poor. One of the women in her company said to her, "O mistress, if you were to give me a small portion of this money, I would buy something with which to break our fast." But Nafisah replied, "Take this thread and sell it, and with that money we will break our fast." So the woman sold the thread, on which the prince had no claim, and used the money to buy bread for Nafisah and her company.

In the *Ketāb al-kawākeb as-sayyārah,* this story is told about Nafisah on the word of Hari:

Nafisa, daughter of Ḥasan, possessed many unusual virtues concerning which numerous stories are told. For example, there is the story of an old woman, extremely poor, who had four daughters she could barely feed. The woman and her daughters made their living by selling home-spun woolen thread which they made during the week and then sold at the bazaar. One Friday, she wrapped the bread in a red cloth, as usual, and set out for the bazaar intending to spend half the earnings gained in purchasing a book for her daughter, and the rest in food for the household.

Enroute, a bird swooped down, seized the package, and flew off. Seeing this happen, the lady fell down in a swoon. Once she regained consciousness, she reflected with anxiety that she would have no money with which to feed her children who would all perish of hunger and poverty. As she sought solace in tears, a crowd of concerned people gathered round her. When she told them her story, they recommended that she visit Nafisa, so that through her prayers, God might assuage her anguish.

Arriving at Nafisa's house, the lady related the episode of the bird and asked Nafisah to assist her with her supplications. Feeling pity for the lady, Nafisa prayed, 'O God! Your power over all is pre-eminent. Your reign prevails over all. Restore to these people what You have seized, for they are Your creatures, Your family, and You are Omnipotent over all beings.' Nafisa then remarked to her guest, 'Sit down. God is powerful over all things.' Though worried about her children's hunger, the lady seated herself and waited for consolation. After an hour had gone by, a group of travellers suddenly arrived at Nafisa's house.

'A strange thing has just happened to us,' they said. 'A party of us were voyaging on the ocean in the utmost peace and safety, but as we approached your harbor our sailing ship developed a hole in the hull. Water began to gush into the ship, and we almost drowned. We tried to stop the leak, but were powerless to do so. Suddenly, a bird carrying a red bundle miraculously flew overhead and dropped it into our vessel. By God's will we used that bundle of thread to stop the leak. We have brought five hundred dinars with us to express our gratitude for having survived.'

Nafisah, crying out, exclaimed, 'O my Lord, my God! How kind and generous You are to Your servants.' She then summoned the lady who owned the thread and asked, 'What would you have sold your thread for?' 'Twenty dirhams,' replied the lady. Nafisah then gave her the five hundred dinars, which the woman, in turn, gave to her daughters. As a result, they put aside their business, and came to wait on Nafisa, seeking her blessing.

Monāwi relates that Nafisa spent most of her time engaged in asceticism, worship, fasting and nightly vigils of prayer. According to his account, she married Eshāq Mo'tamen, the son of Ja'far Sādeq, and then travelled to Egypt where she died in 823. She was widely reputed for her saintliness and charismatic powers.

It is said that as the hour of her death approached, Nafisa was fasting and people encouraged her to break her fast. She remarked, "How strange a request! For thirty years now, I have aspired to meet God while fasting. Is it now time to break my fast? No! Impossible!" She then began to recite the sura *An'ān* 'Cattel'. Upon reaching the words, "They have an abode of peace with their Lord" (VI: 127), she passed away.

Nafisa had already had her grave dug, and had performed within it six thousand complete recitations of the Koran. After her death, great mourning pervaded Egypt. Candles were lit, people from villages and towns gathered together to commemorate her, in every house in Egypt the sound of lamentation and weeping could be heard. Prayers were pronounced for her sake, and much grief was expressed. Great crowds collected for the funeral ceremonies, the like of which had never before been seen in Egypt. She was buried in her house in Darb Samāh, near Cairo.

The tomb of Nafisa is famous for its efficacy in granting prayers. Although her husband wished to bury her remasins in Medina, her fame had spread through the Egyptian populace, and their desire to have her tomb in their land prevailed. She was buried in a district called 'The Gate of Wild Animals' *(Darab sabā')* near Cairo. It is said that he had a dream in which the Prophet told him, "Do not debate with the Egyptians concerning Nafisa, O Abu Eshāq, for through her grave, Divine Mercy will favor them." (Nabahāni, *Jāme' karamāt al-auliyā'*)

حکایات چنان شد که حکما انچه در کتب خیران بوده اند و حکما و پیان شو نپشته اند کرده
نجاصیت قایل شده اند جابر حکمتش را گفته روزی بسر بگریبان تفکر فرو برده بود و متامل نشسته
حضرت امام صادق بر او آمده پرسید که در چه کاری عرض کرده که میخواهم که تحقیق کنم که از
جرنده و خزنده و پرنده کدام بیضه می نهد و کدام بچه می آورد امام فرموده که محتاج باین تعداد

5

Ja'far Ṣādiq conversing with a woman. From the *Majāles al-'oshshāq* (dated 1552) in the Shirazi Style. Bodleian Library Ms. Ouseley Add. 24 (Ethé 1271), f. 19b.

THE WIFE OF RABA QAYSI

The wife of Rabā Qaysi is said to have spent all of her nights engaged in prayer. When a quarter of the night had passed, she would reproach her husband for sleeping and urge him to rise for prayers, but he would refuse to get up. Again and again during the night, she would approach her husband and admonish him to rise to pray. Still he would not respond. With the approach of dawn, she would approach him again, and say, "O Rabā, the night's armies have gone now. Yet still you sleep. I wish I knew who caused me to be deceived by you, since you are a tormentor and stray from the True Way."

It is recounted that the wife of Rabāh one day picked a dry stick from the ground and commented, "By God, the world is less in value to me than this stick."

It is said that after performing the night prayers, Rabā's wife would clean and beautify herself and change her clothes, then approach her husband and ask him if he had any wish. If he answered no, she would re-clothe herself as usual and stand till dawn praying. (Sha'rāni, *Tabaqāt al-kobra,* Vol. I, p. 56)

THE SISTER OF BESHR AL-ḤAFI

Beshr al Ḥāfi (d. 841) was a Sufi, as well as an authority on *ḥadith.* "I learned piety from my sister," Beshr al-Ḥāfi declared, "she always strove to perfect her life without relying on the labor or produce of mortal beings." (*Ṭarā'eq al-ḥqā'eq, II, 218)*

When the sister of Beshr al-Ḥāfi came to visit Imam Ebn Ḥanbal, she asked him the following question, "We engage in spinning cotton on the roof by the light of the Pure Ones (*tāheriān)* which falls on us while we are working. Is this permissible in your eyes or not?"

Aḥmad Ebn Ḥanbal asked the lady her name.

"I am the sister of Beshr Hāfi," she replied.

Aḥmad Ebn Hanbal pronounced, "True piety shall come from your family. Do not spin cotton in that light." (*Resāla-ye Qoshairi)*

THE WIFE OF HATEM AṢAMM

Ḥātem Aṣamm[1] (d. 852), it is said, once desired to go to fight in the holy wars for four months. He asked his wife, "How much of a stipend should I leave behind for you?"

"Leave as much as will keep me alive," she responded.

"Life is not up to me," pleaded Hātem.

"And neither is daily bread, " his wife reminded him.

After her husband had gone off to the wars, a woman inquired of her, "How much of a stipend did Hātem leave for you?"

She answered, "Ḥātem was but a consumer of daily bread; but the provider of daily bread is here with me." ('Aṭṭar, *Tadhkerat al-auliyā')*

[1] A pupil of Shaqiq Balkhi. See 'Aṭṭār, *Muslim Saints and Mystics,* pp 150-52.

'ABDO'LLAH 'ANBARI'S SLAVE GIRL

'Abdo'llāh 'Anbari offers the following account of his slave girl:

> Once I was deeply enamored of a slave girl whom I owned. I awoke one night and did not find her by my side. I looked over in the corner, and saw her praying aloud, saying, 'By virtue of Your love for me, free me.' I admonished her, 'Don't say, By virtue of Your love for me. Rather say, By virtue of my love for You.' But she rebuked me, saying, 'O lazy man, His love for me has directed me from infidelity to faith and has illumined my eyes with understanding of Him, while your eyes were asleep.' I replied, 'For God's sake, I free you'. She then said, 'Concerning me, you were wrong. Up to this point, I drew two wages, but now only one wage remains.' (Ebn Jawzi, *Ṣefat aṣ-ṣafwat*)

THE SISTER OF ḤALLAJ

Ḥosain Ebn Manṣur Ḥallāj possessed a sister who professed manhood[1] upon the Sufi way and was quite lovely in appearance. When she entered Baghdad, she concealed one half of her face with a veil and left the other half bare and unveiled. A gentleman encountered her and asked, "Why don't you veil your entire face?"

[1] *Da'wi-ye rajuliyat:* that is to say, she claimed to have, *vis-à-vis* her fellow male mystics, an equal rank in regard to her abilities, vigor, and vitality in the spiritual quest,

"First show me a man so that I might veil my entire face," she replied. "There is only half a man in all Baghdad and that's Ḥosain (Ebn Manṣur Hallāj). If it weren't for his sake, I wouldn't even cover this half." (Rāzi, *Marmuzāt-e Asadi dar mazmurāt-e Dāwudi,)*

ABO'L-ḤASAN MAKKI'S DAUGHTER

'Abdo'llāh Ebn Aḥmad Ebn Bakr offers the following account of the daughter of Abol'-Ḥasan Makki, "This fine woman was even purer in piety than her father, spending only three dirhams a year, money which her father earned for her by selling date palm leaves." Ebn Rawāsel Tammār, a neighbor of Abo'l-Ḥasan Makki, recounts the following story about Abo'l-Ḥasan and his daughter:

> I was about to depart on the *pilgrimage* to Mecca, but first paid a visit to Abo'l-Ḥasan Makki to ask him if he had any business for me to perform for him in Mecca. He handed me an envelope and bade me to look up the address of the girl written upon it and deliver the enclosed letter to her. I sensed that he was speaking of his daughter. I took the envelope with me and when I reached Mecca sought out the girl, who seemed very preoccupied with her religious devotions. Indeed, she was famous despite her chosen obscurity. In an attempt to gain virtue's reward, I wanted to donate to her some of my own wealth, but I sensed that if I gave her money outright, she would reject it. So I opened the envelope and to the three dirhams I added fifty more. I resealed the envelope so that it was identical in

appearance as before and delivered it to her.

After I introduced myself, she questioned me for news, to which I replied that everyone was well. At once she remarked, 'Ah, my father has entangled himself with worldly people and has left off his quest for God.'

I insisted it was not so, and then she addressed me, 'By God and by the person for whom you've made the pilgrimage, I want to ask you something. Speak truthfully, please.'

'Ask,' I said, 'I'll tell you.'

'Have you mixed any of your own money with this?'

'Yes, I did,' I rejoined. 'But how did you know?'

'My father would never have sent more than three dirhams,' she confessed, 'because he can't. That is, unless he put aside his devotions, I know he couldn't have sent me more than three dirhams.'

To these words she added in rebuke, 'Now take it all away. You have bothered me much, while you might have done a good turn.'

'How is that?' I begged.

'Because I shall not make use of anything that does not come to me either through my own labor or my father's work. I will not take any money whose origin is unknown to me.'

'Well,' I suggested, 'then take only the three dirhams which your father sent you and leave me the rest.'

'If I only knew,' she demured, 'which dirhams exactly were mine I would take them, but all the coins are so intermixed that I cannot tell. So I will take none of them and will sustain myself until next year by consumming leftovers and scraps gleaned from other people. This will suffice as food for me this year when I am hungry. If you have nothing further to annoy me with, you may go home now.'

Immensely dejected, I returned to Basra and looked up Abo'l-Ḥasan. I told him about the incident with his daughter and begged his pardon. Yet he too refused to take the money back, objecting that the coins were mixed with coins not his own.

'You have deprived both of us of our sustenance,' he added in reproach.

'But what do I do with this money?' I begged.

'I don't know,' he said.

I entreated him repeatedly in desperation, asking what I should do with the money and begging his forgiveness. At last he relented. He suggested I spend the sum on charity. So I did. (Ebn Jawzi, *Ṣefat aṣ-ṣafwat*)

THE DAUGHTER OF OMM ḤASAN ASADIYA

This woman is accounted one of the Sufis of Basra. Sofyān Thawri relates the following account of his visit with her:

When I visited the daughter of Omm Ḥesān Asadiya, I saw imprinted on her forehead the mark of much prostration in prayer, a mark usually found on the knee. I advised her that if she wouldn't visit 'Abdo'llāh Shehāb herself, I would send him a letter so perhaps he would be charitable enough to bestow some of his wealth on her so as to better her living conditions.

'Up until now, Sofyān,' she rejoined, 'I had

respect for you in my heart. Now God has made me devoid of that as well. So, Sofyān, you would beckon me to long after the world from one who is not its true owner.'

At night, she would enter her prayer chamber and close the door. Then she would confess, 'O Lord, each person with their own particular beloved has secluded themselves, and I have retired with You alone. No words, O Beloved, are left to me. Those who disobey You will gain only Hellfire.'

Three days after I had tried to help her, I visited her again. I could see that hunger had taken its toll upon her, so I scolded her, saying, 'O daughter of Omm Ḥasan, you shall not be granted more than was apportioned to Moses and Khezr, as the scripture says of them: "So they departed, until, when they reached the people of a city, they asked the inhabitants for food, but they refused to receive them hospitably." (Koran XVIII:77)

'Sofyān,' she bade, 'say All praise is God's (*al-ḥamdo'lelāh).*'

I said it, and then she replied, 'So you have admitted your gratitude to Him. Thus it is incumbent on you that each time you awake to the meaning of your gratitude, you must reconfess your thanks. In the same way, one must give even further praise for every two thanskgivings, and so on *ad infinitum.*'

Hearing this, I seemed to lose my knowledge, and my tongue was as though it were tied. I wished to rise and leave her, but couldn't. Finally she commented, 'O Sofyān, man's ignorance is quite enough that he should never become proud of his knowledge. The fear of

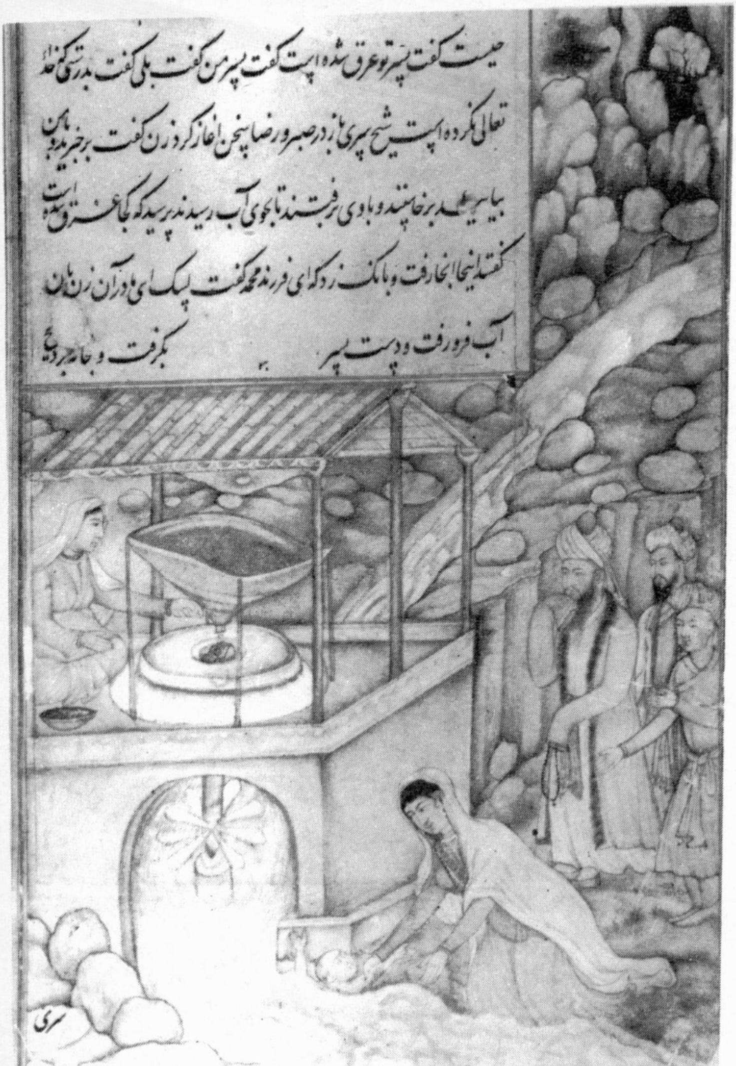
چیست گفت پسر تو غرق شده است گفت پسر من گفت بلی گفت پدر تسلی کن خدا
تعالی نکرده است شیخ پیری باز در صبر و رضا سخن آغاز کرد زن گفت برخیزید و با من
بیایید شیخ برخاستند و با وی برفتند تا بجوی آب رسیدند پرسید که کجا غرق شده است
گفتند اینجا آنجا رفت و بانگ زد که ای فرزند محمد گفت لبیک ای مادر آن زن با آن
آب فرو رفت و دست پسر بگرفت و جامه
سری

6

Tinted drawing illustrating the story of Omm Moḥammad and Sari Saqaṭi in the *Nafaḥāt al-ons* by Jāmi, copied for Akbar at Agra, dated 1605. B. L. Or. 1362 f. 392a.

God is sufficient knowledge for man. Hearts shall never be preserved from corruption until there is a unity in one's efforts on the way of God.' Sofyān commented, "I swear to God, I saw myself as very insignificant indeed."(Ebn Jawzi, *Ṣefat aṣ-ṣafwat*)

OMM MOḤAMMAD, THE DISCIPLE OF SARI SAQAṬI

Omm Moḥammad was a disciple of Sari Saqaṭi. Because of her responsibilities, she sent her son to be taught by a tutor. The tutor, however, sent him to a mill where he fell in the water channel and drowned. The teacher came to Sari and informed him what had occurred. "Come with me to visit his mother," Sari beckoned.

Together they went to the woman, and Sari began addressing her first on patience *(ṣabr)* and then on contentment (*reḍha)*.

"What is your intent behind all this talk, O Master?" asked the lady.

"Your son," Sari Saqati told her, "has drowned."

"My son," she cried.

"Yes," said Sari.

"Surely God hasn't done this," said the woman.

Sari began to speak again of patience and acquiescence. The woman beckoned to him to follow her, and together they rose and approached the water channel. "Where was the spot he drowned?" she asked.

"Over here," the tutor indicated.

The woman walked to the spot and called out, "O

son of Moḥammad!"

"Yes, mother" replied the boy. The woman descended to the bank of the channel and took her son's hand and they went home.

Sari Saqaṭi approached Jonayd and questioned him concerning the significance of the incident. Al-Jonayd pronounced, "This woman fulfills every obligation God has placed upon her. The verdict concerning such a person is that nothing will ever befall her without her prior knowledge. The death of her son was not communicated to her before, thus she apprehended that nothing of the kind had occurred and denied it, knowing that God had not done such a thing." (Jāmi, *Nafaḥāt al-ons)*

THE WOMAN ON THE NILE[1]

Once when I was wandering by the banks of the Nile, I encountered a slave girl who was praying as follows:

> *O You who accompany, inspiring the words of*
> *every tongue!*
> *O You who accompany the hearts of those who*
> *remember You!*
> *O You who are near to the thoughts of those who*
> *praise You!*
> *O You who are the hope of those who languish: I*
> *have realized that I am nothing.*

Upon ending her lament, she shrieked loudly and fell down in a swoon. (Ebn Jawzi, *Ṣefat aṣ-ṣafwat)*

[1] The following twelve stories are attributed to the famous Sufi Dho'n-Nun Mesri (ed.).

THE WOMAN ON THE ROAD TO EGYPT

On the highway between Jerusalem and Egypt, I beheld a person of awesome presence approaching me in the distance. I felt inspired in my heart to question the stranger. As the person came closer, I discerned an old woman dressed in a woolen cloak, clutching a cane in her hand. When I asked her where she was from, she said "From Allah!" I asked where she was going, she said "To Allah!"

I emptied my pockets to give her all I had. But she waved her fist before my face and scolded me, "O Dho-n-Nun! Such an action merely betrays your feeble intelligence. I work for God. I never take anything less it is from Him and I never desire anything but Him." So saying, she departed. (Hojwiri, *Kashf al-mahjub,* p. 126)

THE GIRL BY THE RIVERSIDE

One day I was walking by the bank of a river beside which stood a pavilion. I went to the water and performed my ablutions. When I finished, my eye suddenly fell on the roof of the pavilion. There, on the balcony, I saw a very beautiful girl. Wishing to test her, I said, "Maiden, to whom do you belong?"

She answered, "When I saw you from afar, Dho-n-Nun, I imagined you were a madman. As you came closer, I supposed you to be a scholar. When you came still nearer, I thought you were a gnostic. Then I looked and saw you to be none of these."

"What do you mean?" I demanded.

"If you had been a madman, you would not have

made ablutions. If you had been a scholar, you would not have gazed on what is forbidden. And if you had been a gnostic, your eye would not have gazed on that which is less than Reality."

So saying, she vanished. ('Aṭṭār, *Tadhkerat al-auliyā'*)

THE WOMAN FROM THE MOQAṬṬAM MOUNTAINS

The news reached me that in the Moqaṭṭam Mountains dwelled a particularily pious lady devoted to God. I desired to visit her, but although I searched throughout the mountains I could not find her.

I finally came upon a community of mystics from whom I inquired of her. They counselled me though, saying, "Would you abandon the fellowship of the wise and make friends with lunatics?"

"Though she may be mad," I insisted, "direct me to her."

They finally relented and replied, "She passes by this way quite often. Sometimes we see that she stands still and cries aloud, sometimes she weeps, sometimes she is silent and sometimes she laughs."

I entreated them to take me to her. One of their company remarked, "I last saw her in such-and-such valley..."

In haste I set out to find her and finally heard a voice lamenting. Approaching closer I perceived a maiden beside a huge stone. When I greeted her, she responded cordially and inquired, "Dho'n-Nun," she cried. "His love has driven me crazy. His ecstasy has torn me into a distraught frenzy. His yearning made me lose my heart."

"Where is the place of yearning located?" I asked.

"Oh Dho-n-Nun" she answered "Love (*ḥobb*) is centered in the heart, yearning in the innermost consicousness (*fo'ād*) and ecstasy (*wajd*) in the superconscious arcanum of the heart (*serr*).

She then collapsed in a swoon, weeping hysterically. When she was once again conscious she confessed, "The intensity of my love causes me to supplicate and pray profusely. And this, Dho-n-Nun, is the custom of lovers."

All at once she screamed loudly and fainted on the ground. I shook her body, but she was dead. (Horayfish, *Op. cit.*)

THE WOMAN IN THE KA'BA

While performing the pilgrimage to Mecca, I happened to notice a lady who was clinging to the curtains of the Ka'ba, sobbing and lamenting with the following words:

My inner screams I open to You
But my distress and wretchedness
I shroud from all but You. You busy me
to the exclusion of all others.

Knowing You, I wonder how anyone
Can again distance themselves
From You? How can anyone who has
Savored the joy of Your gracious kindness
Again refrain from You?

She then began to talk to herself:

> At first I treated you moderately, O self, but you paid no heed. I overlooked your errors, yet you were unabashed. Even when the sweetness of prayers was removed from you, you remained unmoved.

When done she began to address the Divine:

> I am utterly nothing, Lord, when I stand before You. You have expelled me from Your service, afflicted me with perplexity and disorientation and deprive me of sensing any sweetness in my devotions. Why have you done this, O You who are the brilliance of my very eyes?

Then she sung out:

> My heart cannot bear separation from you, for nothing is more painful and bitter than separation. Long have I feared what now suffices me: this division between us wrought by separation.

By now I had completely forgotten that I was in God's House and also overlooked the fact that the woman was wearing a *chaddur.* She suddenly reproached me, saying "Close your eyes, Dho'n-Nun. It is forbidden for you to look on me." Her words made me remember that she was female. Trying to excuse myself, I said, "I swear your words so preoccupied me that I was totally unaware that you were a woman."

Her only answer was to say, "Why should God pardon you? Are you not aware that God has certain servants who never occupy themselves with anything besides Him, nor remember anyone but Him?" (Ebn Jawzi, *Şefat aş-şafwat*)

THE LADY IN THE RUINED CONVENT

Upon hearing of a pious lady of ascetic temperament, renowned for her perseverance and struggle on the Sufi way, I formed a desire to meet her.

With this in mind, I discovered that she resided in a ruined convent, spending her days fasting and her nights awake in prayer. I sought her out and stayed nearby. She always seemed active, exhibiting no laxity whatsoever in her devotion. Once, as night fell, I heard her supplicate, "My Lord does not sleep or slumber, how then can His slave sleep? For if the Master if awake, a slave should not sleep. Upon Your Glory and Majesty, I swear, tonight I cannot sleep."

In the morning, I gave her my greetings and she saluted me back. "How can you live in this dilapitated convent," I inquired, "and yet possess such a spiritual state?"

"Don't utter such inept words, Dho'n-Nun," she reproached me. "Lift up your head. Contemplate the heavens. Can you see elsę but the glory of God?"

"No," I admitted.

"Aren't you afraid, being all alone here?" I questioned.

"My heart holds no place for ought besides Him. I have surrendered my heart utterly to His love and my breast overflows with His spiritual mysteries. His knowledge runs through my very veins. Nothing but Him fills my body. How should I not feel intimate in His remembrance, since I am perpetually engaged with Him?"

I begged her to guide me upon the true way and indicate the direction to Divine Unity. For I swear by God, "I am floundering in an sea of sin."

"Take piety as your only provision, Dho'n-Nun," she advised, "and make the hereafter the aim of your quest. Adopt as the vehicle of your journey, asceticism and abstinence from all things. Distance your heart from the world. This will enable you to return to your Creator. Choose to emulate the manner of God-fearing folks. Abandon the way of sinners, until your name be registered in the book of unitarians and you see, by God, that no veil intervenes between you and Him and His doorkeeper no longer rebuffs you."

Her advice affected my heart deeply and caused me to turn back to my Creator. Then she turned her back on me and strolled away, singing He is the Beloved who has promised us union. By Him I swear that my heart is never separate from Him. If you sing His name in my ear, you will make me merry. I would give up my soul to one who mentions my beloved on his tongue. He is the Beloved. There is nothing similar to Him in the world or in my heart when He appears there. It is no marvel if I were to die in the way of love out of yearning for Him. (Horayfish, *Op.cit,* Jāmi, *Nafaḥāt al-ons*)

THE LADY FROM THE DESERT

While travelling through the desert one time, I met a holy woman. When she came closer to me, I saluted her and she returned my greetings.

"Where are you coming from?" she inquired of me.

"I have just come from paying a visit to someone who is so wise that no one else can be compared to him."

"Alas," she exclaimed, "Why have you separated yourself from him, when he is the loving host of strangers?"

Her reply wounded my heart and I began to weep.

"What is this crying for?" she demanded.

"Crying is a medicine," I told her. "It began to act on my pain, so I hurried to assist it."

"But if you were truly sincere," she rejoined, "you wouldn't have cried at all."

"Why do not the sincere cry?" I inquired.

"Indeed they don't," she replied. "Because crying bestows tranquility upon the heart, which is a deficiency in people of wisdom. You are obviously a lazy man."

"Counsel me further," I entreated, "Something that will profit me before God."

"How sorry for you," she remarked. "Didn't your friend help you even as much as to at least allot you needlessness from pursuing superfluous things?"

"I seek you out," I told her, "so that you may teach me something that I might do."

She then advised me as follows:

> When you want to see your Lord, serve Him, for He has one day in store for His friends in which He shows Himself to them. From the goblet of His love, He sates His lovers in this world with Himself, and they never thirst thenceforth.

She then broke down in sobs and lamented, "My Lord, until when shall you forsake me in a dwelling in which no one assists me in my tribulations."

So saying, she went on her way, murmuring, "If the love of the King is in a servant, to what other physician should he refer to cure his sickness?"

THE WOMAN IN THE ANṬAKIAH MOUNTAINS

During one of my trips in the Anṭākiah Mountains, I saw a girl wearing only a woollen cape, who appeared to be insane. She responded to my greeting and asked if I was Dho'n-Nun Meṣri.

"God forgive you," I replied. "How did you recognize me?"

"I recognized you through that knowledge which is aquired through Divine Love." she rejoined. "I want to ask you a question," she pleaded.

"Ask," I responded.

"What is generosity?"

"Forgiveness and charity," I replied.

"But this is merely generosity in the world," she objected. "What is generosity in religion?"

"Haste in obedience to God," I pronounced. "Whenever you make haste to obey God, He knows what is in your heart, and you then wish nothing from Him."

"Too bad for you, Dho'n-Nun." she countered. "For twenty years now I've longed to ask Him for something, yet I feel embarrassed before Him, fearing I might be a bad sort of laborer seeking only money for her work. Still I perform His work, out of veneration and devotion for His sublime majesty."

Then she turned away and left me. (Ebn Jawzi, *Ṣefat aṣ-ṣafwat)*

THE BLACK GIRL

One day when I was out walking, I saw a black girl being stoned by a bunch of children. They were calling her, "the infidel who claims to see God."

I followed her as she moved away and then she called out to me by my proper name.

"How did you know me?" I inquired.

"The clothes of His friends," she pronounced, "are a sign through which the members of His army are familiar with one another."

"What were those children saying to you?" I asked.

"What were they saying?" she repeated.

"They say that you claimed to behold God."

"True," she asserted. "For, ever since I knew Him, I have not been veiled." (Jāmi, *Nafaḥāt al-ons*)

THE TRAVELLING WOMAN

Once while journeying I encountered a lady whom I questioned concerning the ultimate reaches of Love *(maḥabbat).*

"Vain man!" she rebutted me. "Love has no bounds."

"Why?" I inquired.

"Because the Beloved has no bounds," she answered. ('Aṭṭār, *Tadhkerat al-auliyā')*

THE WOMAN BY THE SEASHORE

I was at the seashore when I saw a woman approaching, wearing an old garment made of woven hair. She looked quite thin and feeble in frame and appeared to be saying something. I stepped nearer to hear her words. She seemed to be sorrow-stricken and filled with melancholy. A gale was blowing and the billows of the sea were cast high in the air, and even the fish were visible.

Suddenly she shrieked and fell down. Upon recovering her awareness, she began to weep uncontrollably, then lamented:

> O my Lord, in this solitude do hermits seclude themselves with You. To show Your grandeur, the fish invoke your name in the watery depths, tumultuous waves pound within vast oceans of water. You are the light of the Heavens in the darkness of the night. The waterfilled sea and the bright moon, all prostrate themselves to You. To each separate thing, You apportion a proper quantity. O intimate Friend of the devout in their seclusion!

Suddenly a desperate scream rose from the woman and she died. This astounded me. Soon other women appeared on the scene, also dressed in hair-cloaks, as the first woman had been. They took her corpse away and washed it somewhere concealed from me. Subsequently, they brought her body back and ordered me to perform the funeral prayers over it, which I did. Afterwards, they turned their backs on me, lifted up the corpse and went on their way. (Ebn Jawzi, *Ṣefat aṣ-ṣafwat)*

DHO'L-NUN'S ENCOUNTER WITH AN UNKNOWN WOMAN

Dho'l-nun asked a woman, "From where do you come?"

"From a group of people whose sides have shrunk back from reclining on their beds, who invoke God in fear and hope." she replied.

"Where are you heading?" Dho'l-Nun inquired.

"I am going towards men who are not distracted by traffic or commerce from the remembrance of God." she said.

"Describe them to me." he begged.

She sung some Arabic verses by way of reply:

> They are a company who have rivetted their attention on God, paying regard to naught else. Their object is their Lord alone—how sublime is their aim: the Everlasting Refuge, the Unique Being. The world with its ambitions and status, its pleasures and offspring, holds no interest for them. They do not seek elegant and soft cloths, nor desire to find a pleasant comfortable place to abide in the land. For the lengthier the distance to his destined waystation appears to the traveller, the speedier will he hasten. Although they dwell in valleys and caves, they are as exalted as others in the world in their elevation. (Kalābādhi, *Kholāsa-ye sharḥ-e ta'arrof,* p. 45)

A MAIDEN ON THE BANKS OF THE NILE

Dho'l-nun recounted: "Once while strolling on the banks of the Nile I beheld a dark-skinned person coming towards me. On closer observation, I saw a black maiden robed in a garment of contentment with God, and a girdle of modesty. She had painted her eyelashes with the collyrium of Divine Love, and walking with a gait full of ecstatic yearning, she sang:

> Oh my Lord, my Master, my Ultimate Desire! O You whose omnipotent will determines my deeds! I take refuge in you from a body that will not stand upright in your service; from the insensitive eye that will not weep for love of you, and from the heart that is not filled with yearning for you. O Master and Soverign! You are the King whose mercy and generosity has ordained the elect, that they might be engaged in your service. You have stolen sleep from the eyes of yearning lovers so that they may face your portal. You are that Monarch who has granted intimacy to his confidants. You have dispatched your Spirit to comfort the sincere. O exalted Refuge of gnostic aspirations! O Goal of all who quest! O Confidant of the souls of spiritual wayfarers! O Light of the eyes of the penitent! O Mercy to the miserable and the oppressed!

Then she entered the main road and continued singing aloud these Arabic verses:

> In the night's darkness, I revel in intimacy with my friend, for one whose eyes languish in love never sleeps. O solitary and unique Beauty, I cannot speak of ought besides Your royal Glory. Beloved! Your love courses through my blood and quickens my flesh and bones. The nectar of your remembrance remains rooted, ineffaceable

from my heart.

Having recited these lines, she cried out and reflected, "By renouncing desires, bodies are made light, for deeds performed without desire for recompense are praiseworthy. O how many bodies, who, for the sake of fulfilling their wishes, have stood on foot all night in prayer! O how many the eyes that weep out of remorse for their sins and errors!"

Then she added,"There is sorrow in visiting one's brothers, for they are also brothers in sadness and grief. But the nature of God's friends *(auliyā')* is not to refuse giving counsel to true believers, concealing their disgraceful deeds."

Having said this she vanished.

A MAIDEN ON THE PLAIN OF BANI ESRA'IL

While passing through the plain of Bani Esrā'il, I encountered a maiden who was filled with yearning for the Truth. Her eyes were upraised in contemplation to Heaven. I gave her greeting of peace, and she replied, "Peace be with you also, O Dho'n-Nun!"

"How did you recognize me?"

Addressing me as a lazy good-for-nothing, she said, "God Almighty created the spirits two thousand years before the bodies. As such, they revolved about the Divine Throne. Those that recognize each other from there join each other's company here, and those who do not recognize each other become opponents. In that field, my spirit knew your spirit."

"I perceive you to be a wise woman," I remarked. "Teach me some of the things that God has taught you."

"O Abo'l Faiḍh," she replied, "set the fire of Justice and Equality over your bodily limbs until all but a pure heart melts away and only God remains in your heart. Then he will allow you to dwell by His doorway and appoint you to a new position, commanding your guardian to be subservient to you."

"O sister," I entreated, "tell me more."

She concluded by saying, "Abo'l-Faiḍh, try to save your soul and rescue yourself while you still have time, take from yourself for the sake of yourself. Be faithfully obedient to God, and remember Him lovingly when you are alone." (Ebn Jawzi, *Ṣefat aṣ-ṣafwat*)

ANOTHER MAIDEN FROM THE BANI ESRA'IL PLANE

"Once I was travelling through the desert of Bani Esrā'il," recounted Dho'l-Nun, "with a companion. We met a woman wearing a garment of sackcloth and a woolen veil, carrying a bar of iron in her hand.

"Peace be upon you," I greeted her, "God have mercy on you."

"Peace be to you also." she replied. "But what have men of God to do with the company of women? May God grant you security."

"I am your brother — Dho'l-Nun" I informed her.

"Indeed! O how wonderful, son!" she exclaimed, "May God grant you a long life."

"Where are you going here?" I asked.

"Whenever I arrive in this town," she exclaimed, "since all its inhabitants are heedless of God's commands, I begin to feel contracted. So I set out in search of some pure unpolluted spot where I may prostrate myself in devotion to God alone, to convene with Him in adoration in my heart. My heart seems to have utterly melted away yearning to envision Him."

Never have I heard anyone mention the Friend in such a lovely fashion," I commented. "Tell me, what is Love *(maḥabba)?*"

"God be magnified!" she protested, "you, a wise preacher, ask such a question of the likes of me? Love at the outset causes intense inner labour until the spirits of those who yearn are purified. Then sweet goblets full of delicious draughts of Love are proffered them to imbibe."

Then she shrieked and swooned.

THE WOMAN WHO WAS THE MASTER OF BAYAZID BESTAMI

It is said that when Bāyazid was asked who his master was, he explained:

> She was an old woman. One day, I was possessed by such ecstasy and yearning and sense of unity that not even a hair of anything else could be found in me. In this selfless mood, I went for a stroll in the desert where I happened to meet an elderly lady burdened with a bag of flour. She asked me to carry the flour for her, but I was incapable of taking it, so I beckoned to a lion to take the load. The lion came up to me and I laid the sack upon its back. I then asked the old lady what she intended to say to the

واین چند رباعی از انجاست
از شبنم عشق خاک آدم گل شد
صد فتنه و شور در جهان حاصل شد
سر نشتر عشق بر رگ روح زدند
یک قطره فرو چکید نامش دل شد
تا ظن نبری که در تنم جانی هست
اندر طلبت نهاده ام سر کف دست
زنجیر سر زلف که در گردن تست

7

Shaikh Majd al-Din Baghdādi preaching to a group of male and female desciples. From the *Majales al-oshhaq* in Shirazi Style dated 1552. Bodleian Library Ms. Ouseley Add.24 (Ethé 1271), f. 55b.

townspeople since I did not want them to apprehend who I was. 'I'll tell them,' she replied, 'that I met a vain tyrant.'

'What are you talking about?' I exclaimed.

The lady explained thus, first asking, 'Has the lion been put to trouble or not?'

'No,' I answered.

'Except for the fact that you burden down those whom God Himself has not burdened!' she objected. 'Is that not oppression?'

'So it is,' I admitted.

'And, despite this,' she continued, 'still you desire the townspeople to know that you have subjected a lion and are a miracle-worker. Is that not vanity?'

'Yes it is,' I confessed. So I repented, experiencing abasement from my former exaltation. Indeed that old womans words performed the function of a spiritual guide and master for me. ('Aṭṭār, *Tadhkerat al-auliyā')*

THE ABYSSINIAN GIRL

Shaikh 'Abdo'l Qāder Gilāni has recounted the following tale:

The first time I set out from Baghdad on a pilgrimage to Mecca, I was still young and decided to go alone. On the way, I encountered Shaikh 'Adi Ebn Mosāfer who was also quite young. He asked me my destination and when I informed him of my intenion of performing the pilgrimage, he asked me if he could accompany me. I told him that I was trying to cultivate solitude, but he rejoined that he, too, was practising solitude. So together we set out.

On certain days we would see an Abyssinian girl standing on the way before us, cloaked head to foot in a veil. She would come very close and peer very intently at my face. At last she asked me, 'O youth, where do you come from?'

'I come from Persia,' I replied.

'You've put me to trouble today,' she informed me.

'How is that?' I asked.

'An hour ago,' she explained, 'I was in Abyssinia and had a vision that God Almighty revealed something to your heart and favored you with Grace such as He had never before bestowed upon anyone. Thus I wished to see you and get to know you.'

'Today I will remain in your company,' she added, 'and tonight we will break our fast together,' and at that, we set off.

Out of propriety, she travelled on one side of the valley and I on the other. At nightfall, a tray came down from the heavens with six wheat cakes as well as vinegar and vegetables. The girl cried, Praise be to God, who has been generous to me and my guests! Every night, two wheat-cakes used to be given to me, and tonight you have given each of us two wheat-cakes apiece.' Then three ewers descended, full of a kind of water, the pleasure and delight of which were unlike any earthly water. Later on in the night the girl took leave of us.

On reaching Mecca, Shaikh Mosāfer, while circumambulating the Ka'ba, had a vision and was thrown back senseless on the ground, so that it appeared to some that he had died. But suddenly I beheld the same maiden encountered previously on our trip standing over him and praying, 'Revive! In the name of Him Who caused you to die.'

A vision subseqently overcame me as I was circling the Ka'ba. A voice addressed my inner self and said, 'O 'Abdo'l Qāder, abandon external solitude and observe the solitude of Divine Unity (*tawḥid).* Seat yourself (in public) so that other people may benefit from you. There are certain of our chosen servants whom We wish to lead to proximity to Us by way of you.'

Suddenly the maiden addressed me, saying 'I cannot understand, O youth, the significance of the sign that today I see visible upon you. Light illumines your brow, and angels have gathered about you to the highest reaches of heaven. The saints from their (heavenly) stations are staring at you in amazement, and all of them have now become hopeful of receiving the like that was granted to you.'

So saying, the maiden went on her way and I never saw her again. (Jāmi, *Nafaḥāt al-ons*)

THE LADY FROM GOLPAYAGAN

Shaikh Najibo'd-Din 'Ali Bozghosh Shirāzi tells the story of a woman from Golpāyagān who used to come to Shirāz to visit him in his home there:

> She was a most cultivated, well-informed lady. On one occasion when she was visiting with us for a few days, I happened to be in tight financial straits. She apprehended my condition immediately. In our house we kept a few storage urns, just in case God sent us any extra grain. The

urns, however, were empty, and I had reset the lids on them so they would remain clean inside until needed. Our lady visitor, supposing the urns full, remarked to me, 'Why don't you use the grain stored in those urns when you are in need?'

'But if they're empty,' she wondered, 'why are their lids in place?'

'So they will stay clean inside from dust,' I replied.

Hearing this, she stood and lifted off the lids from the urns, saying, 'The reason for the urns' emptiness is that, with their lids on, they resemble lips tightly shut; when the tops of the urns lie off, then they resemble hungry mouths open to intake food. God, the Almighty, will send food for them, as the proper sustenance is sent for each thing at the time of its need. The food of these urns is grain and cereal; when it is evident that their stomachs are empty, they will be filled with nutriment.'

At once the spiritual mastery of that woman revealed itself, for soon thereafter the Almighty sent us enough grain to fill all the urns. She belonged to the friends of God. (Jāmi, *Nafaḥāt al-ons*)

THE WOMAN IN SHEBLI'S ASSEMBLY

During Shebli's assembly, it is said, an elderly lady once shrieked outloud, disturbing the Shaikh. He expressed his displeasure by saying, "Die, O you who are under the veil!"

"Here I come to die," replied the old lady. So saying, she stepped forward and surrendered her soul.

A cry went up among the multitude collected there. Shebli stood up and went to his house, and for an entire year did not emerge, commenting, "An old woman has crushed my neck." ('Aṭṭār, *Tadhkerat al-auliyā'*)

WOMEN AT THE KA'BA

Moḥammad Ebn Marwān, who was a Sufi and a man of piety, renders the following account:

> I was one day standing under a certain pillar in the Ka'ba. The pilgrims circling the stone were few in number. I noticed four women whose faces radiated spiritual grace. The superior among them clutched onto the black stone repeating an Arabic verse with contrition and abjectness. 'My pilgrimage is not to a house or a rock, my circumambulation is not a ritual revolving around walls.' Then she raised her head and cried, 'O my God! My yearning for You on Your way has made me distraught, and my ecstatic love of You has rendered me totally bewildered. Here I stand before You. If my sins, O God, have caused my rejection by You, yet the ardor of my love has pulled me thus far to the portal of Your House. If my misdeeds have separated me from You, yet the hope that I have in Your generosity has drawn me close toYou. And if my wrongdoing has constrained me, yet my sincere aspiration to reach You has freed me. 'O God! When will I be united with You? When will I be at one with Your glorious beauty? O Friend of the fearful, Companion of lovers and Refuge of the distressed! O Pardoner of sinners! O Absolver of the penitent! O Most Merciful,

pity me out of Your kindness! Envelop me in Your Grace! '

So saying, she stood up and turning her face to the heavens uttered two verses 'Oh Lord, I ask you to forgive my trespasses, my sins, and pursuit of pleasures. Forgive me, O Lord! O merciful one—most merciful of the merciful—I have grasped the cord of hope in you.'

So saying, she sat herself down in sorrow.

The second most senior lady now rose to her feet, staggered forward in agitation, and with protracted sadness, cried, 'O Ultimate End of all aspiration! O Inspirer of the righteous to good deeds! O kindler of the lamp of Divine Love in the hearts of gnostics! O Comrade of the fearful, Doctor of hearts, Forgiver of sins! In yearning to behold Your Face, my body has melted away! I feel ashamed to stand before You, O Most Merciful, have mercy on me and forgive me!'

Then she engaged herself in the following supplication:

'I come unto you complaining of pain and torment; for in you, oh heart-holder, lies my remedy. I have no one else besides you unto whom I may complain, who will see and have mercy upon my weeping. O, forgive me!—Joy of all nature, through your compassion—in one healing look cast your mercy upon me.

The intensity of the woman's ecstasy finally bewildered her, and she sat down in a daze, entranced and consumed in her passion.

The third lady now stood up, weeping copiously and in a loud voice uttered the following prayer, 'O my God! My sins have sent me away from Your doorway! Through my own forgetfulness I have fallen far from You.

Destitute and lowly, I stand before Your portal, wishing You to absolve my impurities and pardon my sins. I flee to You from You. I stand now before Your face.'

Heaving a forlorn sigh, she sang out: 'I come and stand, O Lord on your portal, having lost hope in all others besides You, You who are the best of providers. Grant me what is worthy of you, That I may partake of the best of your provision, for unless I die out of longing to encounter you never shall I attain my aim.' She then, to,o returned to her seat, her eyes heavy with tears.

The fourth lady now stood on her feet, and expressed her remorse, begging God's forgiveness for her sins, 'You have ordered seekers to stand at your threshold in adoration, yet I never imagined myself in their number. O God, never would You have afflicted lovers with sin unless forgiveness was one of your attributes. O my God, if my hopes for Your forgiveness exceed my merits, You are the One Who can pardon me with the vastness of Your Mercy. O, to You no secret thing is hidden! O, Effusive Bounty, Constant Mercy! Forgive my sins which I have concealed. You are the End of my quest. You are He whom I seek.'

Then she supplicated 'Have mercy on me, O sovereign of creatures! You are my refuge, my Lord and Patron. If my errors have caused me to fall far from Your court, my hope in you gives me certainty, for my trust in you is well-placed, expecting your grace and kindness.

Moḥammad Ebn Marwān concludes, 'I was filled with joy at what I had heard, while their spiritual reflections and counsels brought tears to my eyes.' (Ḥorayfish, *Op. cit.*)

THE WOMAN IN THE DESERT

A devout lady found herself separated from her caravan and stranded in the midst of the desert. She wandered hither and thither and finally paused to take her bearings under a thorn-bush. Ruefully she laid her weary head upon her knees and prayed, "O God! I am a stranger, sick and sorrowing, a heart-burnt mendicant!"

At once, from the Invisible World, she heard a voice reply, "Though I accompany you, still you are afraid? Why should you pine or feel alone? I am here, present in your heart, your soul's Confidant."

This verse might have described her state:

Even if these human creatures everywhere
oppose me,
It is fine, my Sweet Friend,
Since You alone, Select One, I adore.

(*Tafsir-e Anṣāri,* I, p. 446)

WOMAN CIRCUMAMBULATING THE KA'BA

Ja'far Kholdi has handed down the following narrative of Jonayd (d. 910):

One year I happened to perform the pilgrimage to Mecca alone. I took up residence in the suburbs of Mecca, and at night I would visit the Ka'ba. One night, while circumambulating the

Ka'ba I saw a girl, engaged in the same ritual, who was saying, 'Love refused to remain hidden. How often did I conceal the love which had pitched its tent in the campground of my heart. When yearning takes over my heart, I engage in commemoration of him. He reveals Himself to me and I disappear, annihilated. Again he revives me, making me rejoice.'

I reproached the girl, saying, 'O maiden, do you not fear God? How can you so boldly engage in this talk in such a sacred spot?'

She retorted, 'O Jonayd, do not step between Him and His friend.' Then she recited these Ara'bic verses:

'Were it not for fear of God, why should you see me abandon sleep? It is Godfearingness that has made me an exile from my homeland. It is ecstasy, you see, which has driven me to flee from selfhood unto Him, as His love has ravished and enraptured me.'

Then she asked, 'O Jonayd do you circle God's house, or do you circle God?'

'I circle the house.' I said.

The girl then raised her head to the heavens and supplicated;

'O God, you are so transcendent, so incomparably pure and abstract! How grand is your Providence to your servants; how exalted is your Sovereignity. People like inanimate minerals revolve around lifeless stone all the while denying those who know the mysteries.'

Then she sang out:

'They circle stones and seek to be close to you although their hearts are more obdurate than any stone. They are bewildered and in their confusion know not who they are themselves. They are all hollow men: the place of contemplative nearness to God within them is void and empty. Were they sincere in love, they would have emptied themselves of the qualities of self, so that by remembrance of God the qualities of Divine Love would be revealed to them.'

Jonayd recounts how he fell unconscious upon hearing her words. After recovering his senses, he discovered she had vanished. (Ḥorayfish, *op. cit.*, Ebn Jawzi, Ṣefat *aṣ-ṣafwa)*

A LADY IN MECCA

Abu 'Abdo'r-Raḥman Maghāzeli related: There was a wise and pious lady who lived near Mecca. One day we went to visit her, and her servant girl announced our arrival, saying that some of her Muslim brothers had come to hear her speak. She cried at first, then turned towards us and said, "Oh my brothers, hold the Day of Judgement present before you in the eye of your heart, and reflect upon what you have done. Desire what you conceive to be acceptable in God's eye for yourselves for you to be accepted on that Day beseeching God to complete his mercy towards you. Try to repair with meritorious deeds those acts which you fear may be blameworthy. Labour to make up your errors and do not forget your souls, for circumstances may change and you will find that things cannot be altered again, and that no ransom will be accepted."

She wept at length. Then, turning to us, she commented, "O my brothers, physical health and sickness all depends on one's good or bad intentions.

O my brothers, the devout have attained Divine Love by means of their love for and exclusive devotion to God. Yet if God and His Prophet had not lent them grace, they would never have attained to this. However, the abstinent love God and His Prophet, and their love for God has caused the faithful believers to befriend them in return for that love. The hearts of the Godfearing have been wounded by the fear of God, drawing them unto God and distancing them from their desires and lusts.

O my brothers, God will deprive you of His graces in proportion to your neglect of his worship, and He will grant you His favor in proportion to your devoted attention to Him. God is grand and ample in His provision." (Ebn Jawzi, *Ṣefat aṣ-ṣafwat)*

THE WOMAN FROM JERUSALEM

"While on the road between Jerusalem and a certain town," recounted 'Othmān Rajāni,"I encountered an old woman. She was dressed in a woolen cape and *chador.* I saluted her and she returned my greeting, asking from where I had come.

"From this village." I answered.

"Where are you going?" she inquired.

"To another village on an errand." I answered.

"How far is it," she asked "from your home and your family?"

"Eighteen miles." I answered.

"You must have an important errand if you are going eighteen miles to perform it."

"Quite so!" I said.

"What is your name ?" she demanded.

“ ‘Othmān,” I told her.

“O ‘Othmān,” she entreated, “why did you not ask the Lord of your village to attend to your need and secure it for you without trouble?”

Not comprehending her hidden allusion, I answered, “There is no rapport between myself and the headman of the village.”

“O ‘Othmān,” she pressed, “what has ruined the rapport between you and Him, and caused a wall to block your quest for Him?”

Sensing now the spiritual sense of her words, I wept.

“What are you crying for?” she inquired, “Is it for something you have done and forgotten, or for something you forgot and now remember?”

“Something I forgot and now remember.”

At that, she pronounced, “O ‘Othmān, exalt God, who did not forsake you despite your heedless wondering. Do you love God”

“Yes,“ I confessed.

“You speak truly?” she demanded.

“Yes, I love God,” I reiterated.

“If you have realized the station of Divine Love,” she inquired,“what has He apportioned you with from His Divine Wisdom?”

Her words bewildered me, and I felt at a loss to answer her.

“Perhaps ‘Othmān,“ the old lady pressed, “you are the sort of fellow that prefers to conceal his love?”

At that I was dumbfounded, and knew not what to say. She commented, “God witholds the rarities of His wisdom and deep love from entering the precincts of idle hearts.”

"I will ask God to have mercy on you, should you supplicate God to embrace me in His Love." I prayed.

She waved her hand contemptously in my face but I persisted in my demand that she pray for me. Then she said, "O servant of God, go on your errand. The Beloved knows what He has given you in your heart." Turning her back on me she reflected, "were it not that I feared the abatement of my spiritual state, I would have related with unabashed pride to you my spiritual attainments." Then she added, "Alas for this yearning and passion which only Your vision can satisfy, this moaning which only subsides through Your grace."

"I swear by God," 'Othmān testified, "I weep whenever I recall this incident." (Ebn Jawzi, *Ṣefat aṣ-ṣafwat)*

THE MAIDEN FROM JERUSALEM

Abu Solaimān Dārāni (d. 830), the great Sufi master, told the following tale which was related to him by a certain Sa'id from Africa:

> While sitting in the company of my friends in a mosque in Jerusalem, I observed a maiden attired in a hair-cloak, with a woolen bonnet on her head, praying as follows, 'O my Lord, O my God! How narrow the way is for one who lacks guidance! How terrifying is solitude to one who lacks a comrade!'
>
> 'Maiden,' I interjected, 'why have men cut themselves off from God?'
>
> 'For love of the world,' she commented. 'Realize, however, that God has certain servants

whom He sates with the ambrosia of His Love, and so infatuates their hearts that they love nothing but Him.' Then she recited these verses:

Prepare your provisions of good deeds for the journey to the hereafter, for it is deeds which will nurture you in the grave. Man is a guest among his own kin. He dwells among them briefly, then departs. (Ebn Jawzi, *Ṣefat aṣ-ṣafwat*)

A LADY IN MECCA

"A certain pious lady once lived in Mecca," Moḥammad Ebn Bakkār has recounted. "She was endowed with such a spiritual state as to cause her to wail and shriek at least once every hour. People pointed out to her that she was possessed by a state unlike that of anyone else and asked her if she wished to be cured of her pain."

"Cure this pain?" the woman cried. "Alas my heart is pierced with pondering about how to remedy it! Do you not marvel that I am still alive, sitting here right before you, yet my heart is a blazing fire of love and yearning for God? And these flames shall not subside until I return to my Physician who knows my cure and possesses the proper salve for my heart. Yet it seems that my long-suffering in this house, in which even weeping provides no relief, serves to satisfy His goodwill." (Ebn Jawzi, *Ṣefat aṣ-ṣafwat*)

A LADY FROM BASRA

"In Basra," writes Sa'id Ebn 'Aṭṭār, "I was informed

that there dwelled a certain devout lady. She was occupied in prayer when I met her. After she finished, she asked my name. When I told her, she declared, 'Anything, O Sa'id, which hinders you from God is inopportune for you.' Then she turned her back on me and reapplied herself to her prayers." (Ebn Jawzi, *Şefat aş-şafwat*)

ANOTHER LADY FROM BASRA

According to the account of 'Ali Ebn Ḥasan, the following supplication was once made by a woman in Basra:

> May you perish, O heart; how neglectful you are that you forgot to remember God's almightiness! Oh My Lord, how shall I ever approach you on the Day of resurrection seeing as hardhearted creatures such as myself are outcast from you. (Ebn Jawzi, *Şefat aş-şafwat*)

A WOMAN FROM AJRAN

'Abd Rabbeh al-Khawwās recounts the following supplication of a woman from Arjān in the province of Fars in Iran:

> O Lord, when I meditate upon the wisdom of Your conduct among your creatures, I perceive that Your justice crushes them. Then I reflected upon myself by the vastness of Your mercy and realized that Your effusive grace embraces every

being. O Lord, You have delayed chastisement of sinners, so Your lack of haste and granting of respite to them has made them desirous of Your gracious forgiveness. An why should it not be like this, since your bounty and grace towards previous peoples and nations was equally generous."

In like manner she continued her supplication, weeping profusely. (Ebn Jawzi, *Şefat aş-şafwat*)

A WOMAN FROM BALKH

Abu Balāl Aswad tells of encountering a woman devoid of possessions or baggage while making the pilgrimage to Mecca. After asking her where she came from and being told that she came from Balk he questioned her further. Below is the account he provides of their conversation:

"I see that you are travelling without any provisions or baggage," I observed.

"I left Balkh," she rejoined, "with ten dirhams, and I still have five left."

"What do you plan to do," I asked, "when no dirhams are left?"

"I will sell this cloak," she responded, "and purchase one that is cheaper, using the remaining sum for personal expenses."

"But if this amount comes to an end," I entreated, "what then shall you do?"

"I will sell this blouse and spend its money."

"But when that expires, what will you do?"

"O idle man," she rebutted me, "I will ask Him to

bestow something on me."

"Have you ever asked Him such a favor before?" I asked.

"How sorry it is for you!" she exclaimed. "I feel ashamed to ask anything of the world from Him while I have more than I need of it."

"Here, mount this donkey and traverse the rest of the road with it," I suggested.

"Saddle him for me." she ordered.

Abu Balāl Aswad concludes his account of the incident as follows:

"I left her and the donkey, and went off as I had some business to take care of. When I retuned, I saw the donkey standing there with its saddlebag full of flour, though I couldn't imagine from where it had come. I looked for the lady but could not locate her." (Ebn Jawzi, *Ṣefat aṣ-ṣafwat*)

A WOMAN CIRCLING THE KA'BA

Abu'l-Ash'abh Sā'iḥ presents the following story of a woman he once saw clinging onto the curtains of the Ka'ba:

> This woman was lamenting, crying out, 'Oh you who are my fear after intimacy, my debasement after my exaltation, my poverty after my riches...'
>
> I addressed her, saying, 'What has befallen you? Have you lost your money? What adversity have you encountered?'
>
> 'No, no,' the girl replied, 'I have lost the heart I once had.'

'And is that your only misfortune?' I inquired.

'What misfortune could be greater,' she replied, 'than to be deprived of one's heart, to sever one's heart from the Beloved?'

'The loveliness of your voice,' I commented, 'prevents me from hearing the pilgrims chanting as they circle the Black Stone.'

'O Shaikh,' she redressed me, 'does this house belong to you or to Him?'

'To Him,' I replied.

'Is the sanctuary yours or His?' she questioned.

'It is His sanctuary,' I answered.

'Then leave me alone,' she concluded, 'to lament my lowliness before God, as much has been permitted to the pilgrims to His house.'

She returned to her lament, saying, 'O my God, by Your Love for me, give my heart back to me.'

'But how do you know,' I interjected, 'that He loves you?'

'He deployed His armies," she replied, "for my sake, going to great lengths to convey me from the house of dualism unto the portal of Divine Unity *(tawḥid)*, thus causing me to know him after having been ignorant. Is this anything less than Divine Grace?'

'But what of your friendship for Him?' I questioned.

'It is the greatest, the most exalted thing,' she responded.

'Do you know Love?' I asked.

'What would I know,' she countered, 'if I did not know Love? Love, if followed in moderation, produces a sweet fruit. However, when Love becomes excessive, a deadly pain and destructive depravity is created. Love is like a tree whose planting is bitterly painful, but the fruit of which is sweet and palatable.'

Then she sang these verses: 'For one restless in love, patience and rest do not exist, for his weeping eyes are open wounds and his limbs grow lean and pine away in love's ardour and grief. Who can remedy the lovers distress, since love is complicated in pursuit of its aim and tends towards annihilation?" (Ebn Jawzi, *Şefat aş-şafwat)*

ANOTHER LADY

Once I overheard a devout lady praying through her tears, related 'Abdo'llāh Ebn Moḥammad. Her words were as follows:

'O God, I am so weary of life, that if I found someone selling death I would buy it out of my ardent longing to behold God and witness the vision of His Face.'

'Are you sure of your deeds?' I questioned her.

'No,' replied the woman, 'but how can He ever torment me with all the love and goodwill I hold towards Him?' (Ebn Jawzi, *Şefat aş-şafwat*)

A WOMAN WHO REALIZED 'RELIANCE ON GOD'

The following story has been told by Ḥasan Ebn Ja'far, on the word of his father:

I passed by a house and encountered a poverty-stricken old woman who was weeping and lamenting as follows, 'O God, how forbearing and forgiving You are! People try to approach You by means of their good deeds. Yet how may I, laden down with sins, invoke You, since I hold no deeds to my name that might please You? Grant me then, O provider, Your own forbearance which will serve to save me from the torment hereafter.'

I asked the lady if she had any children. When she told me she didn't, I asked her who lived with her.

'God be magnified!' exclaimed the woman, 'A being dwells with me with whom I am preoccupied. What is there to fear when God is your friend and confidant?'

Her words caused me to cry. I inquired how she supported herself.

'Don't talk about things that are futile,' she objected. 'I have gotten to this age without availing myself of the likes of you or anyone else. Haven't you read in the Koran, "and He Himself gives me to eat and drink, and whenever I am sick, heals me?" ' [XXVI:79-80] (Ebn Jawzi, *Şefat aş-şafwat)*

THE WOMAN IN THE DESERT

I once met a maiden in the desert, related Abu Moḥammad Morta'ash, and had the following conversation with her:

"O lady, where do you hail from?" I asked.

"From my homeland."

"Where are you going?" I asked.

"To my home."

"Where are your provisions?" I inquired.

"That One who has summoned me forth grants my provisions because I have trusted in Him."

"Don't you have any water?" I asked.

"Only those who fear thirst take water along," she said.

"Have you no mount to ride upon?" I asked. "The journey is long."

"On the contrary." she responded, "Instead of one mount I have four, yet you are veiled and cannot perceive them. My first mount is that of contentment, upon which I sit whenever God's Providence besets me. Next, when adversity arrives, I ride upon the mount of patience and exercise forbearance. Thirdly, when I am favored by Divine Grace, I sit upon the mount of gratitude and praise God. Lastly, whenever I am blessed by God's Love, I mount the steed of yearning." Or she may have said, "When I am granted the grace of devoted obedience to God, I mount the steed of sincerity."

Turning heavenwards, the maiden lamented, "O Lord, Your love has consumed my soul, driven me from house and home and made me an aimless wanderer."

I saw that the maiden was crying and asked her why she wept. "Yearning pulls me," she answered. "The Friend is absent. My heart is love-crazy and indifferent to itself. Since such is my state, how can there be any comfort or peace of heart for me?"

"What is the true way to the Transcendent?" I finally inquired.

"To seek for the Beloved through the heart upon

8

A tinted drawing of a darvish and her dog. Mughal 1750. B.M. 1955-10-8019.

the scales of the Invisible World." (*Ferdaws al-morshediya,* p. 92)

THE LADY IN THE IRAQI TAVERN

'Abdo'l-Wāḥed Ebn Zayd recounted, in Basra, news reached me of a female devotee who had become wildly distracted in love, and could be found in one of the city's taverns. I spent three days searching for her in vain. On the fourth day, I happened to notice an emaciated woman, dressed in a threadbare garment wearing a necklace, who was staring at me .

"Who are you looking for, Abo'l-Wāḥed?" she inquired.

"You," I said.

"Do not look for me," she replied.

"Why not?" I asked.

"Because for fifteen years now my soul has been seeking my heart and has not yet found it. My innermost consciouiness sought my spirit and found no trace of it," she explained, "so then 'Abo'l-Wāḥed why did you bother to come?"

I asked her to give me spiritual counsel. "How strange!" she mocked. "Here is a physician who claims to cure others, while he himself is sick. O 'Abo'l-Wāḥed, you preach to people, urging them to turn to God, yet your words have no practical benefit for yourself. So how can my counsel ever help you?"

"God bless you!" I cried. "I am subject to a pain which physicians are impotent to cure and suffer from a wound which all surgeons despair of ever healing."

"O 'Abo'l-Wāḥed," she retorted, "if you place the whip and the scourge of Divine Love and the saw of intense longing upon your limbs, everything which has been concealed from you in your soul will come to light.

"But leave me, O brother, for you have distracted me from speaking the truth. O Beloved, I take no delight in the remembrance of God (*dhekr)* as do those 'who have believed and whose hearts have attained serenity in the remembrance of God. Verily in the remembrance of God do hearts find rest!' (Koran XIII:28) Those who are serene are believers in the remembrance of God. Those who experience the ardor of longing find serenity through God. Yet the serene ones are still subject to Divine retribution, because their remembrance causes them delight and sensual pleasure, becoming, hence, a veil. So the soul (*nafs)* is veiled, the heart is in error, the innermost conscience (*serr)* is grief-stricken, while the spirit is the desired object. The soul (*nafs)* is full of animosity, the heart is engaged in Koranic recitation, the innermost conscience relishes its salubrity, while the spirit is exalted.

When the soul ails, its cure is prayer and fasting. When the heart languishes, its cure is contentment, solitude, penitence, and meditation. When the innermost conscience is afflicted, its remedy is constancy in God, and abstinence from all else but God. The way to the Divine Majesty is beset with terrors. Contemplation bestows awareness, and aspiration allows you to concentrate your attention.

The soul may occupy itself with remembrance of the Friend, seeking guidance to the truth, but no way to Friend is opened except by the Friend's will. Likewise, the heart may be engaged in revelation through contemplation, but no way is opened except by the Friend, and innermost conscience may be united in communion with the Friend, but no one can have a glimps there without the Friend will

Beware! God Almighty will deprive the heart of the servant who has desires, of sensing any sweetness in their devotions. Whover is so deprived, will become blemished in soul, and veiled in heart. Thus their soul's only gain will be pain, and their heart's sole benefit will be suffering. *(Bustan al-arefin wa tofeh al-moridin,* p. 286)

BIBI HAYATI KERMANI, POETESS AND MYSTIC

In the early part of the nineteenth century, a certain noble woman by the name of Bibi Ḥayāti was born into a family with a long tradition of Sufism, in the town of Bam, in the Kermān province of Iran. She was raised under the supervision of her brother Rawnaq 'Ali Shah, a Shaikh of Nur 'Ali Shah (one of the masters of the Nimatullahi Order). Perhaps it was due to his guidance that her contemplative life later acquired such brilliance.

In the early years of her maturity, she was taken by her brother to attend one of the Sufi gatherings of Nur 'Ali. The spiritual light of his presence apparently caused a change of state in her and awakened an intense ardor for spirituality within her. Shortly thereafter, she was initiated into the Nimatullahi order. Progressing gradually but steadily in both the esoteric development *(sayr)* and exoteric ethics *(soluk)* of the Sufi path, Hayāti succeeded in acquiring virtues of both a spiritual and secular nature.

Eventually, the relationship between master and disciple exerted a further attraction over Hayāti, and she fell under the sway of the lightning flash of human love. Soon afterwards, she married Nur 'Ali Shah, then master of the Nimatullahi Order. In her own eloquent words:

> The arrow of my supplication reached the target of Nur 'Ali Shah's acceptance. An aurorial breeze wafted to my soul where the whiteness of the sun of the true dawn broke. The sun of his loveliness, in whose atmosphere the bird of my soul soared like a moth of dancing light, suddenly shone forth. My outcast eye opened to the light of his world-adorning countenance.

Ḥayāti's Sufi life, in conjunction with the wife-husband relationship, only served to further perfect her poetic and spiritual nature. She became a rhapsodist in the orchard of love and affection.

Knowing his wife's poetic inclination, Nur 'Ali Shāh finally requested that she try her hand at verse. As Ḥayāti writes in the introduction to her *Divān*, "One day that king in the climes of gnosticism, that guide in the lands of heart and soul, parted his pearl-strewing lips while in the midst of conversation and declared:

> If you must adorn yourself, you should become a diver in the profound ocean of rhetoric, breaking open the pearl-laden oysters of verses, till you gird about yourself an ode of decorative jewels.

In an attempt to excuse herself, Hayāti insisted

that she was neither a man of letters nor of the pen.

"But being a lover," replied Nur 'Ali Shah, "is the work of men, since the seeker of the Lord is male.[1] In the realm of love, sincerity, and Sufism, you too are a man. True manhood is courage. The real man is one who never retreats, who remains constant once he has put down his feet in search of perfection."

Following her master's command, Hayāti set her hand to compose a *Divān* of poems, which eventually came to constitute a remarkable collection of profound and beautiful verses. Reviewing her collected poems, it appears that Hayāti was perfectly acquainted with both the exoteric and esoteric (or mystic) sciences. She adhered both to the external principles of her religion and to the fundamentals of Sufi gnosticism.

In addition, she possessed a highly practical nature and a talent for domestic organization. She was accomplished not only in the ways of Love, but often demonstrated her capacity as a warm-hearted caretaker and cook for her Sufi brothers and sisters.

To give her justice, it might be said that it is only a lady endowed with such noble character and qualities who would be suitable as the spouse for the Pole (*Qotb*) of his age, Nur 'Ali Shah.

Insofar as can be gathered from her poems (in particular her "Ode to the Cupbearer," *Sāqi nāma*), Ḥayāti was perfectly acquainted with the conduct of *Samā'*, as well as the different varieties of Persian musical scales.

---

[1] An Arabic proverb (ed.).

Ḥayāti bore Nur 'Ali Shāh a daughter by the name of Ṭuṭi, and it is said that she, like her mother, possessed a command of literature and was given to the expression of mystical subtleties.

Ṭuṭi eventually married Sorkh 'Ali Shāh, one of Nur 'Ali Shāh's disciples from Hamadān. Ṭuṭi's youngest son was Sayyed Reḍhā, one of the renowned Shaikhs of the Nimatullahi Order. At age sixty-five, God bestowed on him a son by the name of Moḥammad Sa'id Khushcheshm, also a renowned Shaikh of the Nimatullahi Order.

Selected Poems of Hayāti

I. Ghazal 56[1]

How ever again will one behold
The moon's glory
If, over the heart his visage beams
blazing, like the sun?
Through the soul, the Turks of his eyes
Ravage, charge, while, those curls of blaspemy,
Tresses of infidelity, subvert our faith.

But once were he to lift the veil
from his face the world would be nullified,
the universe stupefied.
He struts, brandishing his upright grace,
His stature, elegant, dandy
Through the garden, mocking the cypresses.

[1] In translation the original order of lines of this *ghazal* has been rearranged to give what seems to be more logical cohesion to the metaphors of the poem.

He charges in a cavalcade
Riding a gnostic steed,
In the hallowed space of Divinity,
Sphere of Sanctity . . .

Tonight the Saki, lips stained red
Like rubies, pours forth wine
To every drunkard's pleasure
To each ecstatic's taste.

Since Ḥayāti has imbibed his ecstasy—
Soul-sated by his pure-hearted wine,
To what fountain of life could she incline?

II. Ghazal 61.

Before a trace could be seen of the chained
lineage of creation, of the ancient concatenation
of this outer world— I carried within me
remembrance of that stray lock of yours,
your tresses' pointed tip . . .
From Invisibility's domain, utterly veiled
your face, brilliant as any sun, sought revelation
Thus these atoms of representation,
these particles of things' phenomena, were cast
into vision.

From the very first moment,
that initial instant of time's breath,
your love: amor deos,
lay an intimate depository within our soul,
treasure in the heart's secret chest.

In the land of your meadows
our soul's lark soared aloft,
homebound on your way
before the sprouting of even a flower
from Possibility's rosebed.

A hundred thanks! . . . within the tabernacle
of Ḥaya̅ti's eyes, your face lies
envisaged, everpresent and lovely.

III. Ghazal 87

Into the precincts, the curtain-bound court
Of sapiental intuition, I've bored a way
Through your Love, burnishing
All the rust clouding the heart's looking-glass.

Long before eternal time's first beginning,
He who was then Emperor, brought me forth,
From Invisibility to Actuality's country,
To let me more intimately know Him. . .

Raptured and wrought, my heart lay tangled
And bound in your curls' involute strands,
Long, long before a sign of any motion bestirring
The chain of being's formative essences could be
perceived.

I've spent a desperate lifetime of search
Asleep at the winehouse door
If only once I might hold in hand
That Grail, in which a vision of all worlds
is beheld.

Saki, Saki, one more chalice, one more glass!
Come, bring us; again these harps,
These dulcimer's incantative whispers
Have bereft my heart.

Only to that spiritual communique
Which from thought of you emanates,
Intimate in my heart's every mystery,
Did I ever incline to listen, or care to speak.

The sun of my being shimmers
Forth again from the aurora of the soul,
Nur Ali— lumin gloria
Forecast upon Hāyati's heart.

IV. Ghazal 96

Is this then the night of Power
Or merely — your hair,
Is this the dawnbreak, or your own face?
In the divan *of Beauty*
Is it an immortal first distich?
Or a mere couplet,
Inscribed from your eyebrow?

Boxwood from the orchard,
Or cypress from the rosegarden . . .?
Is it the tuba tree, date-bearing in paradise
Or your own stature — elegant, empathic . . .?
Is it that odor of musk carried by Chinese deer,
Or rosewater's delicate scent?
Is it the rose's wafted breath,
Or the qualities of your perfume?

Is this a scorching lightning bolt,
Or fire radiant from Mt. Sana'i?
Or my burning sigh,
Or your innate character?

Is this Mongolian musk,
Or unadulterated ambergris?
Is it your hyacinth curl
Or your braided tress?

Is this a chalice of the red wine of dawntide
Or White Magic?
Your narcissus-like eye, in a drunken stupor
Or your sorcery?

Is it the garden of Eden
Or an earthly paradise —?
Is it a Ka'ba of the heart's masters
Or your back street?

Everyone faces to pray
A qibla *of adobe and mud,*
The gibla *of Hayāti's soul*
Is turned towards your face.

V. Ghazal 13

Every breath every instant, why
Do you rip this sword of spite across my chest,
Till when shall you bathe my grief-stricken flesh
in blood?

Like the fabulous Chinese deer
My heart, in your tresses' twisted kinks

is ensnared. . .
Ah, do not let your cruel dart,
Bathe in blood my deerlike heart.

Enter, what of it?
Tonight, my dwelling-place, cottage of grief
With your union elate
This grief-ravished soul.

Don't break my rhyme's jewels
For they're nourished on the gut's blood,
Raised on an inner anguish —
Why crush such precious pearls?

Since in your quarter
Ḥayāti kneels in dust
With your Grace caress
This woman of dust.

VI. Ghazal 38

His visage like tulips,
His temper fiery, his faith wine.
Sprightly, a wild juniper in grace
Reckless in his gallantry,
Drunken in this ecstasy.
His ruby lips devoted to wine,
His curls were kinks of hyacinth,
A seductive violence in his narcissus eyes,
His approach: bloodthirsty coquettry.
Then, teeth clenched, and lips locked
His blood throbbing, his heart pounding
He arrived at my bedside one midnight. . .

His lips parted then
Like rosebuds opening to speak
"Oh you, who are in ecstasy unconscious
Drunk on the Cup of my human display —
Whoever has lost his eyes to Love
What dream of sleep, what mind for food
Can his bosom still sustain?
How happy the lover
Who never stoops down, on the first step
To food or sleep. . ."

From the consorts of paradise
Who shall seize Heaven's wine?
Whoever like Ḥayāti, was intoxicated with God
Before the beginning of time.

BIBLIOGRAPHY

Aflāki, Shamso'd-Din Aḥmad, *Manāqeb al-'ārefin.* 2 vols., Ankara, 1959-60.

'Ameli, Bahā'od-Din Moḥammad, (Shaikh Bahā'i) *Kolliyāt-e Shaikh Bahā'i.* Edited by Gholām Ḥosain Jawāheri. Tehran, n. d.

Anṣari, Khwaja Abdo'llāh . *Tafsir-e 'erfāni va adabi-ye Qor'ān-e majid.* Edited by Ḥabibo'llāh Amuzegār. Tehran, 1968.

_____*Manāzel as-sā'erin.* Incl. *'Elal-e maqāmāt.* Edited by S. Laugier de Beaurecueil. Cairo, 1962.

_____*Ṣad Maidān.* Incl. *Manāzel as-sā'erin.* Edited by Rawān Farhādi. Kabul, 1976.

_____*Ṭabaqāt aṣ-ṣufiya.* Edited by 'Abdo'l-Ḥayy Ḥabibi. Kabul, 1968.

Arberry, A.J., trans. *The Doctrine of the Sufis.* Cambridge University Press, 1977. Partial translation of Kalābādi's *Kitāb at-ta'arrof li-madhhab ahl at-taṣawwof.*

_____trans. *The Koran Interpreted.* Oxford University Press, 1983.

_____trans. *Muslim Saints and Mystics.* London, 1976. Partial translation of 'Aṭṭār's *Tadhkerat al-auliyā'.*

Aṭṭār, Farido'd-Din. *Elāhi-nāma.* Edited by Helmut Ritter. Tehran, 1980.

_____*Khosraw nāma.* Edited by A.S. Khañsāri. Tehran, 1969.

_____*Moṣibat-nāma.* Edited by Nurāni Weṣāl. Tehran, 1977.

_____*Tadhkerat al-auliyā'.* Edited by Moḥammad Este'lāmi. Tehran, 1975.

_____*Manṭeq aṭ-ṭair.* Edited by Sayyed Ṣādeq Gauharin. Tehran, 1977.

Austin, R. W.J. *Sufis of Andalusia.* London, 1971.

Baqli, Ruzbehān. *Sharḥ-e Shaṭḥiyat.* Edited by Henry Corbin. Bibliothèque Iranienne, 12. Tehran, 1966. Rpt. 1981.

Dehkhodā, 'Ali Akbar. *Loghāt-nāma.* Compiled under supervision of Moḥammad Mo'in. Tehran, 1947-73.

Ebn 'Arabi, Moḥyiyo'd-Din. *Foṣuṣ al-ḥekam.* Edited by Abo'l-A'lā 'Afifi. Beirut, 1980.

_____*Fotuḥāt al-makkiya.* 4 vols. Cairo, 1911.

_____*Ruḥ al-quds* and *Al-Durrat al-Fakhira.* Trans lated by R.J. W. Austin as *Sufis of Andalusia.* U.K.: Beshara Publications, 1971.

Eṣfahāni, Abu No'aim, *Ḥelyat al-āwliyā'.* 10 vols. Cairo, 1932.

Hayāti, Bibi. *Divani Hayāti.* Edited by Dr. Javad Nurbakhsh. Tehran, 1970.

Hojwiri, 'Ali ebn 'Othmān. *Kashf al-maḥjub.* Edited by V. A. Zhukovsky. Leningrad, 1926.

Ḥorayfish, Sho'aib al-. *Ar-rawḍh al-fā'iq.* Cairo 1850.

Jāḥeẓ, Abo'l-'Othmān. *Al-Bayān wa't-tabin.* Cairo,

1933.

Jawzi, Abo'l-Faraj Abdo'r- Raḥman Ebn. *Ṣefat aṣ-ṣafwat*. Haidarābād, 1976.

_____ *Solwat al-ahzan*,

_____ *Shodur al-Oqud*

Jawzi, Sebṭ Ebn. *Mer'āt al-zamān*, MS. 1505, Bibliotheque Nationale, Paris.

Jami, 'Abdo'r-Raḥman. *Nafaḥāt al-ons*. Edited by Mehdi Tauḥidipur. Tehran, 1964.

Kalabādhi, Abu Bakr Moḥammad. *at-Ta'arrof le-madhab ahl at-taṣawwof.* Persian translation by Moḥammad ebn 'Abde'llāh Mostamli Bokhārā'i. *Sharḥ-e Ta'arrof,* 4 vols. Lucknow, 1912. The author has used a Persian commentary on this text: *Kholāṣa-ye Sharḥ-e Ta'arrof.* Edited by Aḥmad 'Ali Rajā'i. Tehran, 1970.

Khallekān, Ebn. *Wafiyyāt al-a'yan.* Cairo, 1899.

Karbalā'i, Ḥāfeẓ Ḥosain Ebn. *Rauḍhāt al-jenān wa jannāt al-janān.* Edited by Ja'far Solṭān al-Qorrā'i. Tehran, 1965.

Kāshāni, 'Ezzo'd-Din Maḥmud. *Meṣbāḥ al-hedāya wa meftāḥ al-kefāya.* Edited by Jalālo'd-Din Homā'i. Tehran, 1946.

Makki, Abu Talēb. *Qut al-qolub fi mu'āmalāt al-maḥbub,* 2 vols. Cairo, 1892-3.

Modarres, Mirza Moḥammad 'Ali. *Rayḥānat al-adab,* 8 vols. n.d. 2nd edition. Tehran, Chop-khana Shafaq.

Monawwar, Moḥammad ebn (al-). *Asrār at-tauḥid fi maqāmāt ash-Shaikh Abu Sa'id.* Edited by Dhabiḥo'llāh Ṣafā'. Tehran, 1928.

Moqaddasi, 'Ezzodin Ebn 'Abdus-Salām Ebn Ghānem. *Sharh hāl al-awliā* (Arabic MS #1641 - Paris Public Library)

Nabahāni, Shaikh Yusof Ebn Esmā'il. *Jāme' karāmāt al-auliyā'.* Bulaq, Egypt, 1911.

Nicholson, R. A., trans. *Kashf al-maḥjub of Al-Hujwiri.* E. J. W. Gibb Memorial Series. Vol XVII. London, 1911; reprint: 1976.

Nishapuri, Abo'l-Qāsem al-Ḥasan Ebn Moḥammad Ebn Ḥabib al-. *Ketāb 'oqalā' al-majānin.* Damascus, 1924.

Nurbakhsh, Dr. Javad. *In the Paradise of the Sufis.* New York, 1979.

_____*In the Tavern of Ruin.* New York, 1978.

_____*Traditions of the Prophet (Aḥādith).* 2 vols. New York, 1981 & 1983.

_____ *Masters of the Path.* New York, 1980.

'Othmān, Maḥmud Ebn. *Ferdaws al-morshediya fi asrār aṣ-ṣarmadiya (Siratnāma Abo'l-Eaḥāq Kāzeruni),* Edited by Iraj Afshār. Tehran, 1954.

Qoshairi, Abo'l-Qāsem. *Tarjoma-ye resāla-ye Qoshairi.* Translated and edited by Badi'oz-Zamān Foruzānfar. Tehran, 1982.

Rāzi, Najm ad-Din. *Marmuzāt-e asadi dar marmurāt-e Dawudi.* Edited by M.R. Shafi'i Kadkani. Tehran 1973.

Sa'di, Moṣleḥo'd-Din. *Bustān.* Edited by by Nuro'd-Din Irānparast. Tehran, 1977.

Sha'rāni, 'a. al-W. *Ṭabaqāt al-kobrā.* Cairo, 1882.

Shirāzi, M.M., *Ṭarā'eq al-ḥaqā'eq.* 3 vols. Edited by M.J. Maḥjub. Tehran 1940.

Smith, M. *Rābi'a: the Mystic (A. D. 717-801) and Her Fellow Saints in Islam.* California: Rainbow Bridge, 1977.

Sohrawardi, Shehābo'd-Din Abu Ḥafṣ 'Omar. *'Awāref al-ma'āref.* Bulaq, Egypt. 1872-3.

Solami, Abu 'Abdo'r-Raḥmān. *Ṭabaqāt aṣ-ṣufiya.* Edited by Johannes Peterson. Leiden, 1960.

Taghribirdi, Abo'l-Maḥāsin Ebn. *Al-Nojum al-zāhira.* Leiden, 1855-61.

INDEX

abad, (post-eternity); 47.
Abada, Mo'ira: see Ofayra Abeda
Abādān; 137.
Abbasid; 22.
'Abdah, Bent Abi Showāl; 20, 56, 57, 58, 149.
abdāl, (subistitutes); 12.
'Abdo'llāh 'Adawiya; 174.
'Abdo'llāh Ebn 'Isa; 19, 20.
'Abdo'llāh Ebn 'Omar; 103
'Abdo'llāh Ebn Moḥammad; 218, 231.
Abo'l Faidh; 210, 211,
Abu 'Ali Faḍhl Ebn Moḥammad Farmādi (d. 1084); 26.
Abu Ali Faqih; 62.
Abu 'Amir; 159.
Abu Sawār 'Adawiya; 175.
Abu Bakr; 4.
Abu Bakr Ebn 'Abid; 90.
Abu Bakr Mofasser; 67.
Abu Balāl Aswad; 228, 229.
Abu Barakāt; 134.
Abu Homān; 140.
Abu Kalāb; 58.
Abu Khaldah; 85.
Abu Khāled Barrād; 181.
Abu 'Othmān; 146.
Abu Sa'id Abo'l-Khair (d.1049); 9, 99.
Abyssinian; 205, 214.
adab (proper manners); 146.
Adam; 49.
'Amer, Abdo'l-Wāḥed Ebn; 42.
Aflāki; 53, 156.
Africa; 147, 225.
Ahari Sufi Order; 167.
aḥwāl, (mystical states); 7, 80.
Aḥwāl, 'Asem; 117.
Ahwaz; 165.
Ajami, Habib (d. 737); 152.
'Aisha (the Prophet's wife); 176.
Al 'Atik; 16.
al-ḥamdo'lellāh, (Praise be to God);195.
'Ali Ebn Abi Tāleb; 2, 4, 49, 181.
'Ali Ebn Ḥasan; 227.
'Ali Zayno'l-'Abidin; 184.
Allah; 3, 6, 132, 198, 195.
Amat al-Jalil; 90, 91.

'Amir, 'Abdo'l 'Aziz Ebn; 97.
'Ammār Rāheb; 173.
'Amr 'Adawiya; 90, 91.
'Amr, Moḥammad Ebn; 21.
'Amru Ja'fi, Ḥafṣ Ebn; 125.
'Anbari, 'Abdo'llāh; 191.
Anṣāri, Isā Ebn Esḥāq; 181.
Anṣāri, Khwāja 'Abdo'llāh (d.1089); 9, 147.
Antākiah Mountains; 205.
'aql, (intelect); 108.
Arab; 1, 2, 13, 40, 47, 93, 102, 125, 130, 168, 204, 208, 213, 216, 217, 221, 223.
Arberry; 5, 50.
Ardabil; 155.
'āref, (gnostic); 59, 100, 124, 163, 169.
Arjān; 227.
Asadi, Boshr Ebn; 78.
Aṣamm, Ḥātem (d. 852); 7, 190.
Asbost; 167, 169, 171, 179.
Asbosti, Bābā Faqih Aḥmad; 167.
aṣḥāb, (companions); 2.
Asku; 167.
Asmā' Ramliya; 101.
'Atā Ebn Mobārak; 100.
'Aṭṭār,Farido'd-Din (d.1221.); 3, 9, 12, 15, 16, 21, 22, 28, 34, 35, 36, 37, 75.
auliyā-ye khodā , (saints of G0d); 3, 12, 33, 206, 210.
azal, (eternity); 47.
Bedouin; 147.
Azdi, Aḥmad Ebn Sahl; 130.
Azerbaijan; 88, 99.
'Azizah; 90.
Baghdad; 61, 66, 134, 160, 161, 187, 191, 192, 205, 209, 213.
Baiḍha; 99.
Bakhār, Moḥammad Ebn; 226.
Bakr, 'Abdo'llāh Ebn Aḥmad Ebn; 188.
Baku'i, Kamāl ad-Din;; 168, 169,172.
Balkh; 92, 93, 94, 227.
Bam; 236.
Bani 'Adil; 91, 175.
Bani Esrā'il; 210, 207.
Bani Makhzum; 121.
barakat, (blessing); 113.
Bardah-ye Ṣarimiya;; 100,
Basra; 16, 17, 19, 23, 24, 25, 26, 27, 43, 45, 61, 94, 100, 101, 128, 130, 149, 153, 165, 173, 194, 222, 223, 226, 227, 230, 233.
basṭ, (expansion) 104.
Baysān; 98.
Bāyazid Basṭāmi (d.874 or 877); 8, 92, 83, 161, 162, 212Bohlul; 115.
Bozgosh Najibo'l-Din 'Ali Shirāzi; 215.
Cairo; 145, 158, 188.
Caliph Mo'āwiya; 130.
Caliphs; 1.
chaddur (veil); 30, 118, 119,

Khushcheshm, Moḥammad Sa'id; 239.
Khwāja Najmo'd-Din Moḥammad; 89.
kofr, (infidelity); 43, 52.
Konya; 167.
Koran; 5, 6, 7, 11, 12, 19, 20, 24, 27, 31, 32, 35, 43, 44, 48, 51, 58, 65, 85, 94, 117, 118, 120, 122, 130, 153, 158, 162, 173, 175, 188, 195, 232, 236.
II: 255; 153.
LI:22; 173.
LIV:55; 32.
LV:3; 58.
LVII:16; 5.
LXXXIX:27-29; 50.
V11:143; 23.
V:119; 43.
V:54; 47.
VI: 127; 184.
XI:I3; 31.
XIII:28; 231.
XLII:19; 173.
XVIII:28; 5.
XVIII:77; 95.
XXIV:60; 116.
XXIV:60; 115.
XXIX:69; 5.
XXVI:79-80; 232.
XXVI:88-89; 5, 120.
XXXIII:35; 12.
XXXVI:88-89; 119.
Kotobi, Ebn Shāker al-; 23.
Kufa; 89, 177, 178.
la elāha ella' llāh,(there is no deity but Allah); 6, 132.
Laylat al-qadr, ('Night of Power'); 96.
madhkur (the One who is remembered); 155.
Maghreb; 136.
Maghāzeli, Abu Abdo'r-Raḥman; 222.
Magi; 2.
Mahdi Ebn Maymun; 118.
maḥabbat, (loving kindness); 7, 47, 70, 80, 206, 208, 212.
Maimun, Abu'l-Ḥasan (d. 845); 78.
Makki, Abo'l-Ḥasan; 192, 194.
makr, (deceit, guile); 31, 59.
malakut, (World of Angels);, 127.
Mālek Dinār; 44, 45, 62, 149, 150, 180.
Malika; 176,
Mālini Sufi;113.
Manbuḍh; 140.
Manqusah; 178.
Manṣur Ebn Moḥammad; 127.
Manzur, Bashir Ebn; 57.
Marchena of the Olives; 144.
ma'refat, (gnosis of God); 15, 16.
Marḥum, 'Isā Ebn; 149.
Marwān Ebn Mo'awiya al-Fazzāri; 78.
Marwān, Moḥammad Ebn;

208, 217, 219.
Marwazi, 'Abdo'l-Mālek Abu 'Abdo'r-Rahman; 180.
Mary; 12, 16.
Mashad; 130.
Mawṣali, Aluf; 86.
Mecca; 18, 23, 24, 25, 58, 86, 95, 144, 119, 121, 130, 145, 146, 156, 157, 161, 162, 165, 166, 168, 169, 183, 184, 192, 200, 209, 210, 214, 216, 218, 220, 222, 224, 226.
Medina; 95, 130, 180, 188, 213.
meḥrāb, (oratory); 50.
Mena;¯84.
Mesma' Ebn 'Aṣam; 55.
Mirzā 'Abdo'llāh; 135.
Mo'ādha; 171.
Mo'ādha 'Adawiya; 153.
Mo'ādh Ebn Fazl; 139.
mo'āmalat, (transactions); 16,
Mo'āwiya; 'Abdo'l-Karim Ebn; 118.
Mobārak, 'Abdo'llah Ebn, (d. 797); 90.
Moḍher; 140.
Moḥabber, Dā'ud Ebn; 150.
Moḥammad; see Prophet Moḥammad.
Moḥammad Ebn Ḥosain; 91.
Moḥammad Ebn Qodām; 121.
Moḥammad Ebn Sa'd Timi; 225.
Moḥammad Sirin; 117.
'Mo'irah 'Abadah; 151.
mojāhada, (spiritual combat); 58, 91, 96, 126, 175.
mo'jezah, (miracles); 33.
mojtahed, (jurisprudent); 101.
mokāshafāt, (visions); 96.
mokhleṣ, (utterly pure); 33.
Molqan, Ebn al-; 22.
Monāwi, Abdo'r-Ra'uf; 22, 187.
Monkader, Moḥammad Ebn; 160.
Monkar; 35, 50.
Moqaṭṭam Mountains; 199.
Morta'ash, Abu Moḥammad; 232.
Mortaḍhā Zobaydi; 21.
Mosamme' Ebn 'Asem; 91.
Mosāfer, Shaikh 'Adi Ebn; 213, 214.
Moses; 24, 33, 195.
Moslem 'Abdi; 151.
Moslem Ebn Yasār; 102, 103.
Mosni, 'Aḥmad; 111, 113, 114, 115.
Mosul; 86, 126.
Mo'tamen, Eshāq; 184, 188.
Mount of Olives; 24, 84.
Mowerreq, Abu; 183.
mowāfeqat, (concordance and compatibility); 70.
Mt. Arafat ; 26.
Mt. Lebanon; 66, 67.
Mt. Sana'i; 24, 228, 242.
muezzin; 156.
Musa, Abu, 86.

rak'ats (unit of prayer); 32, 68, 94.
Ramadan; 96, 118, 119.
Rāshed Ebn 'Alqamah Ahwāzi; 122.
Rawnaq 'Ali Shah; 226.
Ray; 92.
Rayhāna; 124.
Rebāt al-Baghdādiya; 132.
reḍha (contentment); 196.
roku', (genuflection);118.
Roqiya; 124.
Rostam Khān Qaraqozlu; 130.
Rowaim, Abu Moḥammad; 54,
Rudbāri ,Abu 'Ali (d.934); 90, 155, 188.
Rudbāri, Aḥmad Ebn 'Atā'; 155.
Ruḥ Ebn Salmah Warrāq; 140, 153.
Rumi, Jalālo'd-Din (d.1273);. 9, 156, 157.
ruzah, (ritual fasting); 6.
Ruzbehān Baqli Shirāzi (d.1209); 9.
sabr, (patience); 196.
Sabzevāri, Ḥājj Mollā Hādi; 1.
Sa'di; 48.
ṣādeq, (sincere); 45.
Ṣahba, Abu; 175, 77.
Sahl Ebn Sa'd; 137.
Sa'di, 'Abdo'llāh Ebn Rashid; 150.
Sa'id al-'Ami;154.
Sa'id Ebn 'Abdo'l 'Aziz; 131.
Sa'id Ebn 'Aṭṭār; 226.
Sa'ih, Abu'l Ashhad; 229.
Sajaf Ebn Manẓur; 54.
Sakhtiyāni,Ayyub; 180.
Saki; 224, 227, 240, 241.
Salām, Abu 'Abid Qāsem Ebn (d. 838); 145, 146.
Salāma 'Abedah; 150.
Salāma Al-Afqam; 150.
Salām Aswad; 122, 123, 124.
salāmat, (well-being); 53.
Salām Ebn Abu Moti'; 62.
Salameh, Moḥammad Ebn; 132.
ṣalāt, (prayer); 6.
Sāleh Ebn 'Abdo'l Karim; 212.
Sāleḥ Meri (d. 790); 21, 23, 49, 50, 128.
Salem, Aḥmad Ebn; 182.
Salmat, Ḥamād Ebn; 172.
Salmān, 'Abdo'l-Aziz Ebn; 150.
Salmeh Ebn Ḥasān 'Adawiya; 173.
samā' (concerts); 127, 128, 238.
Samiṭ 'Ajlān; 63, 64.
Sanā'i (d.1131); 9.
Sāqi nāma (Ode to theCupbearer); 238.
Sardrud; 167.
Sari Saqaṭi (d. 867); 83, 103, 104, 110, 111, 196, 197.

Ṣarimiyah; 98.
Sarrāj; 127.
Satan; 8, 85.
Sayedi Khwājegi; 171.
sair, (esoteric development); 236.
Sayyed Reza; 238.
ṣedq, (sincerity); 44.
sekhā,(generosity); 58.
Separdus, Ḥāji Qāsem; 168.
sett al-foqarā,(mistress of the dervishes); 126.
Seville; 159.
Seyyed Aḥmad; 125.
Shabestari,Maḥmud(d.1339); 9.
Shāfe'i; 4.
shafaqa, (compassion); 156.
Shāh, Ne'mato'llāh, (d.1430); 4, 9, 152.
Shaikh 'Adi; 206.
Shaikh Abo'r-Rabi' Mālaqi; 163.
Shaikh Abu Bakr Bokhāri; 125.
Shaikh Ali Khosrowshāhi; 179.
Shaikh Najib ad-Din 'Ali Bozgosh; 215.
shams (sun); 13.
Shaqiq Balkhi (d. 809);. 44, 45, 101, 190.
shaṭḥ (paradoxical aphorism)155.Shaybān Rā'i; 72.
Shebli; 8, 60, 216, 217.
Shehāb, 'Abdo'llāh; 194.
Shekkar Khātun; 171.
Shiraz; 135, 215.
Shi'ite; 2, 3, 4, 130.
Sho'aib Ebn Moḥarrez; 150.
Showāl, 'Abda Bent Abi; 19, 146, 156.
Sindi; 118.
sirr (superconscious arcanum of the heart);50, 200, 235.
Sofyān Ebn 'Aiyana; 78, 94.
Sofyān Thawri (d.778); 23, 42, 43, 50, 53, 54, 56, 57, 59, 62, 71, 72, 89, 90, 194, 195, 191, 196.
Solami; 7, 116, 137.
Solami, Abu 'Abdo'r-Raḥman Moḥammad; 90, 146.
Solaimān, Ja'far Ebn; 152.
Sorkhāb; 99.
Sorkh 'Ali Shah; 238.
Sultan Qarā-Yusef (d. 1433); 169,
suluk, (exoteric ethics); 226.
sunni, 1, 3, 4.
Sura An'ām; 184,
Surat al-Ḥamd; 158.
Syria; 84, 120, 129, 216.
ṭa'at, (obedience); 81.
tāba'in, (followers); 3, 15, 117.
Tabriz; 89, 99, 167, 168, 169.
Ṭafārah; 150.
Taghriberdi, Abu'l-Mahāsen; 22.
tahajod, (night prayers); 104.

ṭāheriān, (Pure Ones); 190.
Tāj ar-rejāl, (Crown of Men); 15.
ṭāleb al-mawlā modhakkar; 12.
Tammār, Ebn Rawāsel; 192.
taqwā, (piety); 6, 15.
ṭariq-e soḥbat, (spiritual companionship); 70.
ṭariqat, (Sufi way); 10, 33.
tawakkol, (trust in God); 72.
tawḥid, (Divine Unity); 13, 52, 55, 145, 203, 215, 226, 230.
Ṭāwus; 125.
Taymiyah, Ebn; 161.
Thābet Banāni; 176.
Tigris; 36, 138.
Tohfah; 101.
Turkey; 167.
Turks; 235,
Ṭusi, 'Abbāsa; 12.
Ṭusi, Moḥammad Ebn Aslam al-; 51, 151.
Tuti; 238, 235.
Wahb Ebn Monyah; 125.
waḥdat al-wojud (The Unity of Being); 9.
Wāḥed Zayd, 'Abdo'l- (d. 793); 22, 19, 31, 63, 64, 123, 150, 151, 177, 178, 233.
wajd (ecstacy); 200.
walāyat, (saintship); 33, 91.
waliya-ye 'āref (spiritual companioness); 165.
weṣāl, (union);52.
wozu', (ablutions); 68.
Yaḥyā Ebn Basṭām; 153.
Yaḥyā Ebn Mo'ādh Rāzi (d. 859); 93.
Yamāmah; 102.
Yamāni, 'Ali Ebn 'Isa; 136.
Yazid ar-Rashk; 177.
Yemen; 125.
Yusef; 147, 165.
Zāher, Malek; 135.
Zatāb, Ḥaji Ḥasan; 171.
Zayd 'Adawiya; 173.
Zaygam, Abu Mālek; 58, 150.
Zobaydi Mortaḍhā; 22, 47.
Zoroastrians; 2.
zohd, (asceticism); 2, 6, 15, 61, 155.